HOLOCAUST MUSEUM

HOLOCAUST MUSEUM

ROBERT FITTERMAN

COUNTERPATH   DENVER   2013

Counterpath
Denver, Colorado
www.counterpathpress.org

Library of Congress Cataloging-in-Publication Data

Fitterman, Robert, 1959–
Holocaust museum / Robert Fitterman.
pages cm
ISBN 978-1-933996-37-0 (alk. paper)
1. Mass media–Philosophy. 2. Photography. 3. Conceptual art.
I. Title.
P91.F54 2013
302.23–dc23
                                        2013008965

This space and time peculiar to the image is none other than the world of magic, a world in which everything is repeated and in which everything participates in a significant context. Such a world is structurally different from that of the linear world of history in which nothing is repeated and in which everything has causes and will have consequences.

−Vilém Flusser, *Towards a Philosophy of Photography*

A woman came with her little daughter
and S.S. men were there one morning
and took the child away:
a mother was forbidden to keep her child with her.

−Charles Reznikoff, from *Holocaust*

auschwitz telephones

     no. 18
     no. 45
     no. 17
     no. 33
     no. 21

−Heimrad Bäcker, from *transcript*

CONTENTS

PROPAGANDA

Propaganda slide entitled "In commercial trades there are 106,699 Jews; In heavy, physical work, only 12,500 Jews." [Photograph #49827]

Propaganda slide entitled "As a member of a foreign race, the Jew in the Middle Ages had no rights of citizenship. He had to live in a ghetto in a separate quarter of the town." [Photograph #49826]

Propaganda slide entitled "The Jew Kutisker swindles 14 million, he plays sick in court." [Photograph #49823]

Propaganda slide entitled "Germany overcomes Jewry." [Photograph #49822]

Propaganda slide entitled "Jewry, Freemasonry and Bolshevism," featuring a poisonous snake with bared fangs, which served as the title slide for Part I of the lecture series. [Photograph #49819]

Propaganda slide entitled "'Ahasver,' the legendary wandering Jew." [Photograph #49818]

Propaganda slide entitled "Throughout history the nations defended themselves against Jewish usury," featuring three medieval depictions of Jewish economic activity. [Photograph #49794]

Propaganda slide entitled "The royal Kaufmann/Haggling Jews." [Photograph #49793]

Propaganda slide entitled "The Court Jew." [Photograph #49792]

Propaganda slide entitled "Criminal-Jew of the 18th century," featuring the image of a Jew named Hoschemeck, who is described in a rhyme as being a tricky criminal who committed seven thefts and deserves to be hanged on a gallows. [Photograph #49791]

Propaganda slide with three images entitled "David and Goliath," "The Victor of Waterloo," and "Atrocity Propaganda." [Photograph #49790]

Propaganda slide entitled "Punishments of Hell." [Photograph #49785]

Propaganda slide featuring a portrait of Henrietta Herz, Gräfin Traiberg, and a scene from the Scroll of Esther. [Photograph #49781]

Propaganda slide entitled "The Titans of Corruption," featuring photographs of five prominent Jews. [Photograph #49770]

Propaganda slide entitled "Stock exchanges/Department stores." [Photograph #49800]

Propaganda slide entitled "The Jews have always been Race Defilers." [Photograph #49796]

Propaganda slide entitled "Karl Marx." [Photograph #49779]

Propaganda slide entitled "Race Defilement," featuring photographs of mixed couples with the slogan: "Women and Girls, the Jews are your ruin!" [Photograph #49776]

Propaganda slide which contrasts a person of mixed race (at the left) with a healthy "Aryan" youth (at the right). [Photograph #49815]

Propaganda slide featuring a series of pictures of religious Jews in various settings in Europe and Palestine. [Photograph #49806]

Propaganda slide entitled "Exploitation," featuring three images: the biblical Joseph selling grain to the Egyptians, a medieval Jewish money lender and modern day brokers on the floor of the stock exchange. [Photograph #49801]

Propaganda slide entitled "Smear Campaign" (Hetze), which portrays the Jew as responsible for inciting world opinion against Germany. [Photograph #49766]

Propaganda slide entitled "The Jew shies away from dangerous occupations." [Photograph #49802]

Propaganda slide entitled "Leading Figures of the System" [Systemgroessen], featuring portraits of six prominent Jewish political and cultural figures in Weimar Germany: Karolina Berg-Rolf, Eugen Levine-Nissen, Hugo Preuss, Walther Rathenau, Georg Bernhard, Isidore Weiss, Rudolf Hilferding and Kurt Eisner. [Photograph #49778]

Page from the anti-Semitic German children's book, "Der Giftpilz" (The Poisonous Mushroom). The text reads, "Well, colleague Morgenthau, we both made another good deal!" "Wonderful, colleague Silberstein! We got good money out of those two goyim and can stuff it into our sack." [Photograph #40011]

Propaganda slide featuring three portraits of mentally ill patients. The caption reads "Idiots!" [Photograph #17574]

Propaganda slide featuring three mentally ill patients. The caption reads "Mentally ill." [Photograph #17566]

Front page of the Muenchner Neueste Nachrichten featuring an article entitled "Jewish murder attack in the German Embassy," about the assassination of Ernst vom Rath, third secretary of the German embassy in Paris by the Jew Herschel Grynszpan on November 7, 1938. [Photograph #58535]

A streetcar adorned with swastikas and a large sign advertising a speech to be delivered by Reichsminister Rudoph Hess on April 7, 1938, in support of the Anschluss. [Photograph #68569]

Propaganda slide entitled "The spreading of the Jews," featuring a map illustrating the expansion of the Jewish population in the 1,500 years since the birth of Christ. [Photograph #49812]

Propaganda slide entitled "The spreading of the Jews," featuring a map illustrating the expansion of the Jewish population from the 17th to the 20th century. [Photograph #49811]

Propaganda slide pertaining to the issue of converting to Catholicism. [Photograph #49782]

Propaganda slide showing the "Jewish spider" entangling Europe in its web. [Photograph #49780]

Propaganda slide showing Dr. Magnus Hirschfeld, founder of the Institute for Sexual Research in Berlin. [Photograph #49775]

Propaganda slide entitled "The Jew in the German Economy," featuring two bar graphs showing the disproportionate influence of Jews. [Photograph #49769]

Propaganda slide entitled "The Jewish spirit undermines the healthy powers of the German people." [Photograph #49821]

Propaganda slide entitled "The Jew a Bastard," illustrating different racial types, and characterizing Jews as a "bastard" race. [Photograph #49813]

Propaganda slide entitled "Destruction of peoples through undermining peasant land laws, usury and collectivization." [Photograph #49807]

Propaganda slide entitled "The Rabbi: 'You ears [of corn] sway back and forth, but business is preferable to you!'." [Photograph #49804]

Propaganda slide entitled "The Sklarek Brothers Dress Company, a million [mark] wholesale enterprise." [Photograph #49824]

Propaganda slide produced by the Reich Propaganda Office showing the opportunity cost of feeding a person with a hereditary disease. [Photograph #07671]

Propaganda slide entitled "Nordic heads [faces] from all periods and countries." [Photograph #49816]

Propaganda slide entitled "13 Jews Daily," featuring a map showing Jewish refugees flocking over Germany's eastern border along with a portrait of Paul Hirsch. [Photograph #49771]

Propaganda slide featuring a deformed infant. The caption reads " . . . because God cannot want the sick and ailing to reproduce." [Photograph #17573]

Propaganda slide featuring a group of mentally ill patients being escorted outside in an unidentified asylum. The caption reads, "Moral and religious concepts of life demand the protection of the congenitally ill." [Photograph #17572]

Propaganda slide featuring two disabled brothers sitting in the grass. The caption reads, "Brothers–asocial." [Photograph #17568]

Propaganda slide featuring two images of physically disabled children. The caption reads, "deformed." [Photograph #17567]

Propaganda slide featuring two photos of mentally ill patients. The caption reads, "Stupid." [Photograph #17565]

Propaganda slide featuring three portraits of mentally ill patients. The caption reads, "Idiotic." [Photograph #17564]

Propaganda slide featuring two doctors working at an unidentified asylum for the mentally ill. The caption reads, "Life only as a burden." [Photograph #17563]

Anti-Semitic cartoon by Seppla (Josef Plank). An octopus with a Star of David over its head has its tentacles encompassing a globe. [Photograph #73815]

Nazi propaganda poster with a picture of a Jewish star and a German caption that reads, "Whoever wears this symbol is an enemy of our Volk." [Photograph #65974]

Untitled anti-Jewish propaganda slide featuring two scenes of Jews in the Berlin Jewish quarter. [Photograph #49829]

Propaganda slide entitled "The Jew avoids work, he lets others do the work for him," that juxtaposes pictures of Jews walking idly through a Jewish quarter and Germans at hard, physical labor. [Photograph #49803]

Propaganda slide entitled "Poison in Film and Theater," depicting the poisonous influence of Jews on German culture. [Photograph #49772]

Front page of the Nazi publication, Der Stuermer, featuring an article and picture of the new "Stuermerbuch" [Stuermer publication], Hofjuden [Court Jews]. [Photograph #37854]

Nazi officials in attendance at the opening of "The Eternal Jew" exhibition in Munich view a segment entitled "Jewish dress was a warning against racial defilement." [Photograph #44201]

Propaganda slide entitled "Jews as rulers of the money markets. 4 Jews in the directorate of the German banking industry." Chairman Georg Adolf Solmssen delivers a speech from the podium. [Photograph #49825]

Propaganda slide entitled "Purim," featuring three images showing Jewish responsibility for catastrophic historical events: the demise of Haman, the terror of the French Revolution and the horror of the Bolshevik Revolution. [Photograph #49808]

One page of an anti-Semitic coloring book with a portrait of a Jew drawn by the German caricaturist known as Fips. The caricature has been colored in. The caption at the bottom of the page reads: "Do you know him?" In the upper left hand corner is the Der Stürmer logo featuring a Star of David superimposed over a caricature of a Jewish face. [Photograph #42034]

Caricature on the front page of the Nazi publication, *Der Stuermer*, depicting the Jewish people as highwaymen poised to drop a large bolder to block the road "to the peace of the nations." [Photograph #37846A]

Members of the SA drive through the streets of Recklingshausen, Germany, on propaganda trucks bedecked with anti-Jewish banners. The banners read: "He who knows the Jew knows the Devil," "The Bourgeois: 'the economy is everything'." [Photograph #80821]

The entrance to the "Eternal Jew" exhibition at the North-West Hall at the Vienna Railway Station. The opening ceremony was presided over by Gauleiter Globocnik and Reichsstatthalter Artur Seyss-Inquart. [Photograph #65597A]

Picture postcard showing a member of the SA waving a large Nazi flag while standing on a mountain ridge overlooking a valley. The postcard was produced by the Julius Schleicher Postkarten Verlag in Leisnig. [Photograph #14954]

Poster advertising the publication of an issue of the anti-Semitic newspaper, *Der Stuermer*, containing a report on a purported case of ritual murder. The text of the poster reads: Ritual Murder is the Saarpfalz: Who was the Murderer? *Der Stuermer* Number 14 presents the shocking documentation. [Photograph #32616]

A poster advertising the anti-Semitic propaganda film "Der ewige Jude" (the Eternal Jew) hangs on the side of a Dutch building. This photograph was taken clandestinely by the donor, Samuel Schrjver. [Photograph #09555]

A group of young German boys view "Der Stuermer," "Die Woche," and other propaganda posters that are posted on a fence in Berlin. [Photograph #86202]

Nazi propaganda slide featuring images of Wilhelm Gustloff, leader of the NSDAP's foreign organization in Switzerland (left), and David Frankfurter, the Jewish student who assassinated him in 1936 (right). [Photograph #49763]

Eugenics poster entitled "The Judaizing of Berlin 1932." The text of the pie charts reads (clockwise from the top): Jews were 42% of all physicians, 52% of all insurance physicians, 45% of all hospital directors, 35% of all dentists, 28% of all pharmicists, 48% of all lawyers, 56% of all notaries, and 80% of all directors of theaters. [Photograph #94185]

Caricature on the front page of the Nazi publication, *Der Stuermer*, depicting the Jew as one who tries to subvert others. The caption reads, "In the pay of Judas / He who subordinates himself to the Jews is only a dwarf never a hero / And he who draws his sword for Judah is never worth the laurels." [Photograph #37860A]

Caricature on the front page of the Nazi publication, *Der Stuermer*, depicting the Jew as the hater of all non-Jews. The caption reads, "Unmasked Hatred / In his unbounded rage the Jew has once again committed a grave error which in our time has undercut him, [and that error is] that he so often displays his hatred against all non-Jews." [Photograph #37857A]

Caricature on the front page of the Nazi publication, *Der Stuermer*, depicting the Jew as the instigator of war. The caption reads, "The beast is on the loose! / A hate brochure which appeared during the war with England." [Photograph #37852A]

FAMILY PHOTOGRAPHS

Prof. Elster poses with his students at the Furstenberg Gymnasium in Bedzin. [Photograph #16586]

The Tichauer family poses for a family photo in the German countryside. [Photograph #57762]

Several Jewish families who are celebrating the holiday of Hanukkah together pose outside a wooden house in Eisiskes. [Photograph #39001]

A group of friends goes sledding in the shtetl. [Photograph #39090]

Group portrait of members of the Hashomer Hadati Zionist youth organization on an outing in the woods. [Photograph #05141]

Prewar portrait of the Kaufman family of Bedzin. [Photograph #57905]

A German-Jewish family poses outdoors for a family portrait with their dog. [Photograph #69297]

Members of five Jewish refugee families look out from the windows of their adjoining apartments. [Photograph #24721]

A group of young people in Eisiskes. [Photograph #39164]

A group of young people pose outdoors in the snow. [Photograph #39631]

Portrait of the extended Szwajcer family in Czerna, Poland. [Photograph #25051]

The first grade class photo of the first coeductional Hebrew day school in Eisiskes. [Photograph #39141]

A Saturday night party at the home of Dina Weidenberg. [Photograph #39262]

Children from the Hebrew School work in the school's garden in preparation for immigration to Palestine. [Photograph #38940]

Young women sew in the workshop of master seamstress Rochel Szulkin. [Photograph #42288]

A meeting of the leadership of Hehalutz Hamizrachi in Eisiskes. [Photograph #39509]

Prewar photograph of an extended Jewish family in Krakow gathered around a table for a family celebration. [Photograph #74921]

Group portrait of the Ovici family, a family of Jewish dwarf entertainers who survived Auschwitz. [Photograph #59966]

Group portrait of members of an extended Jewish family at a family gathering. [Photograph #08488]

Two members of the Ovici family, a family of Jewish dwarf entertainers who survived Auschwitz, perform on stage. [Photograph #47553]

Family portrait of the Brandt family. [Photograph #21997]

Group portrait of Jewish youth in the Dabrowa Gornicza ghetto. [Photograph #07131]

Fourth grade class picture. [Photograph #40640]

BOYCOTTS

Boycott signs posted in the window of J. Neumann Cigarren, a Jewish-owned tobacco store in Berlin. [Photograph #07426]

SA men put up a sign on the front of a Jewish business which reads: "Not one penny to the Jews." [Photograph #29032]

An SA member instructs others where to post anti-Jewish boycott signs on a commercial street in Germany. A German civilian wearing a Nazi armband holds a sheaf of anti-Jewish boycott signs, while SA members paste them on a Jewish-owned business. [Photograph #73811]

Public notice, issued by the Central Committee for the Defense against Jewish Atrocities and the [Jewish] Boycott, instructing Germans to protect themselves against the Jews by boycotting Jewish businesses and Jewish professionals on April 1, 1933. [Photograph #14955]

Boycott signs and anti-Semitic graffiti on the store-front of Pelikan Apotheke, a Jewish-owned pharmacy in Berlin. The graffiti reads: "This Jew is still insolent!" [Photograph #07424]

A crowd of Germans is gathered in front of a Jewish-owned department store in Berlin on the first day of the boycott. Signs exhorting Germans not to buy from Jews are posted on the storefront. [Photograph #78589]

Announcement issued by the Nazi organization in Celle calling upon local citizens not to shop in the Jewish stores listed below. The handbill also forbids NSDAP party members to represent Jews in court, to vouch for Jews in any way, to collect funds offered by Jews for party purposes, to meet with Jews in public or socialize with them in pubs, and to wear party insignia while working in Jewish-owned businesses. [Photograph #43234]

SA pickets distribute boycott pamphlets to German pedestrians. The sign held by one of them reads: "Attention Germans. These Jewish owners of [five and dime] stores are the parasites and gravediggers of German craftsmen." [Photograph #77490]

Reichsminister Joseph Goebbels delivers a speech to a crowd in the Berlin Lustgarten urging Germans to boycott Jewish-owned businesses. He defends the boycott as a legitimate response to the anti-German "atrocity propaganda" being spread abroad by "international Jewry." [Photograph #44203]

Members of the SA block the entrance to the Jewish-owned Erwege store on Fackelstrasse to enforce the April 1 boycott of Jewish businesses. [Photograph #37350]

A woman reads a boycott sign posted in the window of a Jewish-owned department store. The sign reads: "Germans defend yourselves against Jewish atrocity propaganda, buy only at German shops!" [Photograph #14337]

A Jewish-owned store is covered with graffiti and plastered with signs of rhyming anti-Semitic verse. [Photograph #78589A]

An SA member stands guard at the entrance to a Jewish-owned store during the April 1, 1933, boycott. The sign next to him reads: "Germans shop in German stores! The Jew is stirring up hate against Germany! Therefore, do not go to Jewish stores!" [Photograph #98519]

SA pickets, wearing boycott signs, block the entrance to a Jewish-owned shop. The signs read: "Germans, defend yourselves against the Jewish atrocity propaganda, buy only at German shops!" and "Germans, defend yourselves, buy only at German shops!" [Photograph #11286]

Two Nazi stormtroopers stand guard in front of the H. L. Heimann store in Bopfingen, to prevent would-be shoppers from violating the Nazi boycott of Jewish-owned businesses. [Photograph #20212]

A flier issued by the Friends of the New Germany to counter American anti-Nazi sentiment and defend German-Americans. [Photograph #02762]

An SA picket stands in front of the Jewish-owned Tietz department store wearing a boycott sign that reads: "Germans defend yourselves; don't buy from Jews!" [Photograph #11300]

Members of the SA take to the streets of Rosenheim to enforce boycott of seven Jewish-owned businesses on the morning of April 1, 1933. Their signs read: "Germans shop in German stores! The Jew is stirring up hate against Germany! Therefore, do not go to Jewish stores!" [Photograph #98520]

Three Jewish businessmen are paraded down Bruehl Strasse in central Leipzig, carrying signs that read: "Don't buy from Jews; Shop at German stores!" The third marcher from the left is Chaim Bleiweiss, the donor's father. [Photograph #20210]

A poster advertising a mass rally sponsored by the German-American Bund to protest the boycott of German goods. [Photograph #02764]

Trimette Langer, an Austrian Jewish refugee, walks along a tree-lined street in Nice. [Photograph #49276]

BURNING OF BOOKS

A member of the SA throws confiscated books into the bonfire during the public burning of "un-German" books on the Opernplatz in Berlin. [Photograph #01622]

Nazi students unload confiscated materials for the public book burning that is to take place on the Opernplatz in Berlin. [Photograph #45032]

View of the Authors and Their Books section in the special exhibition "Fighting the Fires of Hate: America and the Nazi Book Burnings" (April 29–October 13, 2003), U.S. Holocaust Memorial Museum. [Photograph #N09571.13]

The public burning of "un-German" books by members of the SA and university students on the Opernplatz in Berlin. [Photograph #01621]

Reich Minister for Public Enlightenment and Propaganda, Joseph Goebbels, delivers a speech during the book burning on the Opernplatz in Berlin. [Photograph #85339A]

Reich Minister for Public Enlightenment and Propaganda, Joseph Goebbels, delivering a speech during the book burning on the Opernplatz. [Photograph #85339B]

The public burning of "un-German" books by members of the SA and university students on the Opernplatz in Berlin. [Photograph #01623]

View of the special exhibition "Fighting the Fires of Hate: America and the Nazi Book Burnings" (April 29–October 13, 2003), U.S. Holocaust Memorial Museum. [Photograph #N09574.05]

View of the special exhibition "Fighting the Fires of Hate: America and the Nazi Book Burnings" (April 29–October 13, 2003), U.S. Holocaust Memorial Museum. [Photograph #N09567.11]

View of the entrance of the special exhibition "Fighting the Fires of Hate: America and the Nazi Book Burnings" (April 29–October 13, 2003), U.S. Holocaust Memorial Museum. [Photograph #N09576.06]

View of one section of the special exhibition "Fighting the Fires of Hate: America and the Nazi Book Burnings" (April 29–October 13, 2003), U.S. Holocaust Memorial Museum. [Photograph #N09575.14]

View of one panel of the special exhibition "Fighting the Fires of Hate: America and the Nazi Book Burnings" (April 29–October 13, 2003), U.S. Holocaust Memorial Museum. [Photograph #N09573.16]

Germans crowd around a truck filled with "un-German" books, confiscated from the library of the Institute for Sexual Science, for burning by the Nazis. [Photograph #71188]

View of a section on censorship of the special exhibition "Fighting the Fires of Hate: America and the Nazi Book Burnings" (April 29–October 13, 2003), U.S. Holocaust Memorial Museum. [Photograph #N09568.16]

View of the Immediate American Responses section of the special exhibition "Fighting the Fires of Hate: America and the Nazi Book Burnings" (April 29–October 13, 2003), U.S. Holocaust Memorial Museum. [Photograph #N09568.03]

View of the Immediate American Responses section of the special exhibition "Fighting the Fires of Hate: America and the Nazi Book Burnings" (April 29–October 13, 2003), U.S. Holocaust Memorial Museum. [Photograph #N09568.01]

View of a display case featuring writers in the special exhibition "Fighting the Fires of Hate: America and the Nazi Book Burnings" (April 29–October 13, 2003), U.S. Holocaust Memorial Museum. [Photograph #N09568.18]

SA members and university students march in a torchlight procession around the bonfire of "un-German" books on the Opernplatz. [Photograph #71182]

View of the Students in the Nazi Revolution section of the special exhibition "Fighting the Fires of Hate: America and the Nazi Book Burnings" (April 29–October 13, 2003), U.S. Holocaust Memorial Museum. [Photograph #N09567.07]

View of a panel of the Students in the Nazi Revolution section of the special exhibition "Fighting the Fires of Hate: America and the Nazi Book Burnings" (April 29–October 13, 2003), U.S. Holocaust Memorial Museum. [Photograph #N09569.11]

Students carrying Nazi flags march around the bonfire of "un-German" books on the Opernplatz in Berlin. [Photograph #68984]

Students and SA members carry piles of "un-German" literature to throw into the bonfire on the Berlin Opernplatz. [Photograph #69031]

Students and SA members carry piles of "un-German" literature to throw into the bonfire on the Berlin Opernplatz. [Photograph #69031]

View of the charred remains of books from libraries in Berlin and Marburg that had been stored in a salt mine near Heimboldshausen, Germany. [Photograph #26325]

THE SCIENCE OF RACE

Detail of the "Science of Race" segment on the fourth floor of the permanent exhibition at the U.S. Holocaust Memorial Museum. [Photograph #N02377]

Visitors on the fourth floor of the permanent exhibition at the U.S. Holocaust Memorial Museum view the display on "The Science of Race." [Photograph #N03933.12]

Propaganda slide entitled "The Jew a Bastard," illustrating different racial types and characterizing Jews as a "bastard" race. [Photograph #49813]

Photographs of a pair of genetically identical twins, taken from a set of slides produced to illustrate a lecture by Dr. Ludwig Arnold Schloesser, director of education for the SS Race and Settlement Office, on the foundations of the study of heredity. [Lecture 1, Card 6] [Photograph #95832]

Family tree illustrating the transmission of musical genius through several generations of the family of Johann Sebastian Bach, taken from a set of slides produced to illustrate a lecture by Dr. Johannes Schottky, researcher in the SS Race and Settlement Office, on human heredity, with special attention to physical and mental disabilities. [Lecture 2, Card 29] [Photograph #95899]

Schematic illustration of fruit fly chromosomes detailing the arrangement of genes for a variety of physical characteristics, taken from a set of slides produced to illustrate a lecture by Dr. Ludwig Arnold Schloesser, director of education for the SS Race and Settlement Office, on the foundations of the study of heredity. [Lecture 1, Card 24] [Photograph #95895]

Chart illustrating the possible coloring of the offspring of purebred black, purebred white, and hybrid Andalusian chickens, taken from a set of slides produced to illustrate a lecture by Dr. Ludwig Arnold Schloesser, director of education for the SS Race and Settlement Office, on the foundations of the study of heredity. [Lecture 1, Card 17] [Photograph #95836]

Chart illustrating the transmission of the genetic traits for tall and (recessive) short stature over three generations, taken from a set of slides produced to illustrate a lecture by Dr. Ludwig Arnold Schloesser, director of education for the SS Race and Settlement Office, on the foundations of the study of heredity. [Lecture 1, Card 19] [Photograph #95893]

Chart illustrating the transmission over three generations of the genetic traits for blue and (dominant) brown eye coloring, taken from a set of slides produced to illustrate a lecture by Dr. Ludwig Arnold Schloesser, director of education for the SS Race and Settlement Office, on the foundations of the study of heredity. [Lecture 1, Card 18] [Photograph #95892]

Chart illustrating the determination of the sex of the offspring from the mating of a pair of fruit flies, taken from a set of slides produced to illustrate a lecture by Dr. Ludwig Arnold Schloesser, director of education for the SS Race and Settlement Office, on the foundations of the study of heredity. [Lecture 1, Card 29] [Photograph #95897]

Chart illustrating the various possible offspring produced by the cross-breeding of two genetically pure strains of the mirabilis jalapa flower, taken from a set of slides produced to illustrate a lecture by Dr. Ludwig Arnold Schloesser, director of education for the SS Race and Settlement Office, on the foundations of the study of heredity. [Photograph #95833]

Schematic illustration of the exchange of genetic information contributed by the mother (white) and the father (black) immediately following fertilization, taken from a set of slides produced to illustrate a lecture by Dr. Ludwig Arnold Schloesser, director of education for the SS Race and Settlement Office, on the foundations of the study of heredity. [Lecture 1, Card 26] [Photograph #95896]

Comparative chart illustrating the probability of mental illness among the offspring of schizophrenics, manic-depressives, and members of the general population, taken from a set of slides produced to illustrate a lecture by Dr. Ludwig Arnold Schloesser, director of education for the SS Race and Settlement Office, on the foundations of the study of heredity. [Lecture 1, Card 26] [Photograph #95898]

Eugenics poster entitled "The racial composition of Jews." The German text reads: "The Jews are a mixture of alien Near Eastern, oriental, Hamite and Negroid races." This poster is no. 55 in a series entitled "Erblehre und Rassenkunde" (Theory of Inheritance and Racial Hygiene). [Photograph #94184]

Crossing-matrix illustrating the probability of various hair coloring and textures among the descendants produced by the mating of two different strains of guinea pigs, taken from a set of slides produced to illustrate a lecture by Dr. Ludwig Arnold Schloesser, director of education for the SS Race and Settlement Office, on the foundations of the study of heredity. [Lecture 1, Card 21] [Photograph #95894]

Illustration (top) comparing human sperm cells and ovum to the thickness of a human hair, and (bottom) the four chromosome pairs of the fruit fly (drosopila), taken from a set of slides produced to illustrate a lecture by Dr. Ludwig Arnold Schloesser, director of education for the SS Race and Settlement Office, on the foundations of the study of heredity. [Lecture 1, Card 12] [Photograph #95835]

Chart illustrating the various stages of the conception of a species of worm: Fig. 1-6, the fertilization of the ovum by the sperm; Fig. 7-12, the formation of a nucleus and the division of the chromosomes; and Fig. 13-20, the division of the primary cell and the building of the multi-cell aggregate, taken from a set of slides produced to illustrate a lecture by Dr. Ludwig Arnold Schloesser, director of education for the SS Race and Settlement Office, on the foundations of the study of heredity. [Lecture 1, Card 13] [Photograph #95834]

Drawing illustrating the non-hereditary modifications to genetically identical plants due to conditions in their respective environments: one grown in the flatlands (diagram 1) and the other in the mountains (diagram 2), taken from a set of slides produced to illustrate a lecture by Dr. Ludwig Arnold Schloesser, director of education for the SS Race and Settlement Office, on the foundations of the study of heredity. [Lecture 1, Card 3] [Photograph #95831]

Eugenics poster entitled "The Nuremberg Law for the Protection of Blood and German Honor." The illustration is a stylized map of the borders of central Germany on which is imposed a schematic of the forbidden degrees of marriage between Aryans and non-Aryans, point 8 of the Nazi party platform (against the immigration of non-Ayrans into Germany), and the text of the Law for the Protection of German Blood. [Photograph #94188]

GYPSIES

Taffeta and cotton skirt worn by a member of a German Sinti (Gypsy) tribe. [Photograph #N00407]

Embroidered shirt worn for special occasions by the donor's father, Gheorge Cioaba, chief of the Calderai, a Romanian Gypsy tribe. The shirt was in his possession during the period 1942–1945. [Photograph #N00420-11]

Two young Gypsy children embrace while a third looks on. [Photograph #66316]

Amanda Nickels (left) and Leah Katz-Hernandez (right) assist the candlelighters at the 2000 Days of Remembrance ceremony in the capitol rotunda. Amanda's participation is in memory of the Sinti and Roma victims of the Holocaust; Leah's participation is in memory of the mentally and physically handicapped victims of the Holocaust. [Photograph #N05168-23]

A Serbian gendarme serving the Serbian puppet government led by Milan Nedic escorts a group of Gypsies to their execution. [Photograph #85181]

View of the Gypsy camp in Lodz. Original German caption: "Zigeunerlager" (Gypsy camp), #137. [Photograph #74532A]

A soldier stands behind two barefoot men. [Possibly a member of the Ustasha militia guarding two Serbs or Gypsies during a round-up.] [Photograph #46458]

Close-up of a Gypsy couple sitting in an open area in the Belzec concentration camp. [Photograph #07078]

A group of Gypsy prisoners, awaiting instructions from their German captors, sit in an open area near the fence in the Belzec concentration camp. [Photograph #74705]

View of the Gypsy camp surrounded by a barbed wire fence. Original German caption: "Zigeunerlager" (Gypsy camp), #137. [Photograph #95253A]

View of the Roma (Gypsy) display featuring a dress from Czechoslovakia, on the fourth floor of the permanent exhibition in the U. S. Holocaust Memorial Museum. [Photograph #N02389]

Ghetto residents lean against the wooden fence outside the Gypsy camp of the Lodz ghetto. Original German caption: "Zigeunerslager" (Gypsy camp), #180. [Photograph #65792]

Detail of the Gypsy wagon and violin displayed on the fourth floor of the permanent exhibition at the U. S. Holocaust Memorial Museum. [Photograph #N02388]

Composite photograph of items of apparel used by female members of a German Sinti (Gypsy) tribe, including two skirts, a blouse, a purse and a pair of shoes. [Photograph #N00506]

A row of boxed files in the International Tracing Service's Incarceration Camp Documents Unit containing 11 binders of the files of Roma (Gypsies) at Auschwitz. [Photograph #43576]

Two children [probably Gypsy] lean against a wall as others line up for food in the Rivesaltes internment camp. [Photograph #62415]

Under the supervision of Romanian guards, Gypsies load the corpses of victims of the Iasi-Calarasi death onto trucks in Targu-Frumos. [Photograph #27436]

A group of Gypsy children sitting on a stoop at the Rivesaltes internment camp. [Photograph #30080]

A group of Gypsy children sitting outside in the Rivesaltes internment camp. [Photograph #30079]

A Gypsy child in Rivesaltes. The photo's original caption reads "Don't touch me!" [Photograph #30081]

A group of Gypsy women and children pose for a photograph outside of a building in the Rivesaltes internment camp. [Photograph #62398]

Four Gypsy children pose for a photograph [probably in the town of Rivesaltes]. [Photograph #62403]

A group of Gypsy prisoners congregate in the Rivesaltes internment camp. [Photograph #62402]

Romanian guards supervise the removal of bodies from the Iasi-Calarasi death train in Targu-Frumos. The man whose back is turned to the photographer is Ion Botez, the Police Commissar of Targu-Frumos. [Photograph #27442]

A Gypsy woman stands by a post in the Rivesaltes internment camp. [Photograph #62405]

A Gypsy rummages through the clothing of a corpse that was removed from the Iasi-Calarasi death train at Targu-Frumos. [Photograph #27432]

A woman takes care of her child in a Sinti (Gypsy) camp in Germany. Pictured is Theresia Seibel with her daughter Rita. At the window is donor's aunt, Nelka. [Photograph #33335]

A Gypsy [girl] kneels before the camera. [Photograph #62406]

Romanian guards arrive on the backs of trucks in Targu-Frumos where the Iasi-Calarasi death train is making a stop on its journey. [Photograph #27441]

Ernst Mettbach testifies as a witness for defendant Wilhelm Beiglboeck at the Doctors Trial. Mettbach stated he and thirty-nine other Gypsies volunteered for sea-water experiments. [Photograph #43039]

Civilians walk among the bodies that have been removed from the Iasi death train. [Photograph #91671]

A German soldier stands guard in front of a castle. Pictured is Kurt Winterstein, a member of the donor's family. He was one of Hitler's personal drivers. When the Nazis found out that his mother was Gypsy they took him out of the army and sterilized him. [Photograph #33333]

Gypsies weaving baskets in the Rivesaltes internment camp. [Photograph #30084]

Under the supervision of Romanian guards, Gypsies load the corpses of victims of the Iasi-Calarasi death onto trucks in Targu-Frumos. [Photograph #27440]

A Gypsy woman stands outside of a caravan with a group of children. [Photograph #33338]

Under the supervision of Romanian guards, Gypsies load the corpses of victims of the Iasi-Calarasi death onto trucks in Targu-Frumos. [Photograph #27438]

Gypsies rummage through the clothing and belongings of Jews whose bodies were removed from the Iasi-Calarasi death train at Targu-Frumos. [Photograph #27431]

Group portrait of a Sinti (Gypsy) family in front of their caravans. Pictured are members of the donor's family: in the middle is donor's grandfather, Johann Winterstein. [Photograph #33343]

Under the supervision of Romanian guards, Gypsies load the corpses of victims of the Iasi-Calarasi death onto trucks in Targu-Frumos. [Photograph #27439]

Two Gypsies remove bodies from the Iasi-Calarasi death train during a stop in Targu-Frumos. [Photograph #27435]

A Romanian guard walks past Gypsies removing bodies from the Iasi-Calarasi death train during a stop in Targu-Frumos. [Photograph #27433]

Local Gypsies, supervised by a Romanian policeman, help remove corpses from the Iasi-Calarasi death train during a stop in Targu-Frumos. [Photograph #27424]

Serbs and Gypsies who have been rounded up for deportation are marched to the Jasenovac concentration camp under Ustasa guard. [Photograph #85799]

Serbs and Gypsies who have been rounded up for deportation are marched to the Kozara and Jasenovac concentration camps. [Photograph #85198]

A Sinti (Gypsy) woman hangs out her laundry while her child plays in front of the family's wagon. Pictured is Theresia Seibel and her daughter Rita. [Photograph #33332]

Two Gypsies collect bodies unloaded from the Iasi-Calarasi death train during a stop in Targu-Frumos. [Photograph #27434]

Gypsies remove bodies from the Iasi-Calarasi death train during its stop in Targu-Frumos. [Photograph #27427]

A Sinti (Gypsy) woman poses with a child in front of a field. Pictured is donor's mother Theresia Seibel, born Winterstein, and donor's cousin Peter Winterstein. [Photograph #33337]

Under the supervision of Romanian guards, Gypsies load the corpses of victims of the Iasi-Calarasi death onto trucks in Targu-Frumos. [Photograph #27437]

First Communion portrait of Rita Reinhardt Seibel (now Prigmore). [Photograph #33342]

Gabriel and Theresia Reinhardt, a Sinti (Gypsy) couple, push their twin children, Rolanda and Rita, along the Domstrasse in Wuerzburg under Nazi escort. [Photograph #58336]

Members of a French-Hungarian Gypsy musical band pose for a photograph with their instruments. Pictured from left to right are: Gabriel Reinhardt (donor's father), Benjamin (donor's uncle), Johan (donor's uncle), a cousin, Ben (donor's uncle), Josef (donor's uncle) and unknown [maybe another cousin]. [Photograph #33339]

An elderly Gypsy woman walks down a street accompanied by two girls. Pictured is donor's mother Theresia Seibel (on the right) with her grandmother and her cousin. [Photograph #33340]

Studio portrait of the Sinti (Gypsy) Theresia Seibel who was a performer in the Wuerzburg Stadttheater. [Photograph #33336]

Close-up portrait of Rita Reinhardt Seibel (now Prigmore). [Photograph #33344]

Members of a French-Hungarian Gypsy musical band pose for a photograph with their instruments. Pictured are members of the donor's family: in the middle, with the cane, is donor's grandfather, Johann Winterstein. [Photograph #33341]

DEPORTATION

View of the SS Gotenland, one of the ships used to deport Jews from Norway to Germany. Only 25 of the 760 Jews deported from Norway survived. [Photograph #89095]

View of the SS Donau, one of the ships used to deport Jews from Norway to Germany. On November 26, 1943, the Donau sailed with 530 Jews aboard, 345 of whom went directly to the gas chambers in Auschwitz. [Photograph #89094]

View of the SS Monte Rosa, one of the ships used to deport Jews from Norway to Germany. Of the 760 Jews deported from Norway by ship only 25 survived. [Photograph #89096]

Picture postcard showing an exterior view of the synagogue in Szeged, Hungary. [Photograph #23538]

Members of a Hungarian forced labor battalion dig in a stone quarry. [Photograph #66080]

Members of a Hungarian forced labor battalion pose on the steps of a building in Zalaegerszeg. [Photograph #66079]

Children photographed by Dr. Feher in Sarospatak just prior to his service in Hungarian-Jewish labor battalion 108/57. [Photograph #34326]

Jews during a deportation from the Warsaw Ghetto. [Photograph #05554]

Jews who have been rounded-up for deportation in the Warsaw ghetto walk along a street to the assembly area. [Photograph #50329]

A large crowd of Jews marches down a street after their round-up in Brussels. [Photograph #65979]

Serbian villagers from the Kozara region who have been rounded up for deportation wait in a transit camp in Prijedor for transport to the Jasenovac concentration camp. [Photograph #46602]

A group of men who have been rounded up for deportation are marched out of town. [Photograph #46599]

Serbian villagers from the Kozara region who have been deported from their homes are assembled in a makeshift transit camp located in a livestock market in Grubisno Polje, Croatia. [Photograph #46567]

A little boy standing next to a train track cries out for help. [Photograph #46547]

View of the Chain Bridge spanning the Danube River in Budapest. In the foreground are the ruins of the foreign ministry in Buda. In the background on the far side of the river is Pest. [Photograph #45644]

School portrait of the fourth form class (8th grade) at the Dohany Street girls school, a public school that was attended predominantly by Jews. Pictured in the front row, third from the left, is Olga Gelb, the donor's mother. [Photograph #26805]

Local Jewish women, photographed by Jewish conscripts in Company 108/57 of the Hungarian Labor Service. [Photograph #17168]

A local Jewish civilian wearing an armband walking near the Hungarian Labor Camp where Company 108/57 was housed. [Photograph #17164]

Group portrait of the leadership of the Association of Hungarian Israelite University Students (Magyar Izraelita Foiskolai Hallgatok Orszagos Egyesulete). Among those pictured are Ferencz Gatner and Siegfried Roth. [Photograph #67068]

Yugoslav women and children are gathered in a wooded area during a deportation action. [Photograph #89853]

View of a major street in Krakow after the liquidation of the ghetto, which is strewn with the bundles of deported Jews. [Photograph #39066]

A Chassidic rabbi walks down a street in Bekescsaba, Hungary, in the company of his folowers. In the foreground is Rabbi Shulem Lezer Halberstam. The donor identifies the other men as Tvi Elimelech (father of the donor and gabbai to the rebbe), Rebbe Ratz Feld and Rebbe Shulem Lezer. [Photograph #12746]

Lily Brod, a Hungarian Jewish woman, leans against a chair on the porch of her uncle's home in Budapest. [Photograph #21366]

A group of vacationers holds up large mugs of mineral water on the grounds of a Hungarian spa. Among those pictured are Ernest and Lilly Brod. [Photograph #21365]

Close-up portrait of the cook Strasser and the company messenger of a Hungarian forced labor brigade. [Photograph #66085]

Close-up portrait of a Jewish conscript in a Hungarian labor brigade, dressed in a winter jacket on a snowy day. [Photograph #66082]

Four young men pose on the steps outside their yeshiva. [Photograph #63710]

Jews from the Warsaw ghetto board a deportation train with the assistance of Jewish police. [Photograph #37287]

A group of men who have been rounded up for deportation are marched out of town (probably by members of the Ustasa militia). [Photograph #46598]

Refugees board a deportation train for labor camps in Siberia. [Photograph #96389]

Portrait of Sandor Guttman in the uniform of a Hungarian labor battalion with his arm in a sling. [Photograph #26723]

View of the quarters of Hungarian-Jewish labor battalion 108/57 at Sianki. [Photograph #34324]

Jewish conscripts in Company 108/57 of the Hungarian Labor Service at forced labor clearing snow from a road. [Photograph #34320]

A local Jewish woman, wearing an armband, who befriended Dr. Adalbert Feher and his fellow conscripts in the Hungarian Labor Service. [Photograph #60155]

Jewish deportees march through the streets of Kamenets-Podolsk to an execution site outside of the city. [Photograph #28216]

Portrait of Imre Rosner as a young child. [Photograph #27419]

Portrait of Abraham and Margit Krausz with their daughter, Klara, in Budapest. [Photograph #27413]

Jewish conscripts in Company 108/57 of the Hungarian Labor Service at forced labor clearing snow from a road. [Photograph #60697]

Portrait of Aladar Barber as a Jewish conscript in a Hungarian labor battalion in Sopronbanfalva. [Photograph #10030]

An elderly man and child who have been rounded up for deportation wait with their luggage at an assembly point in the Krakow ghetto. [detail of w/s 02144]. [Photograph #02145]

A Jewish family climbs the stairs to the train platform at the railway station during a deportation action from the Krakow ghetto. [Photograph #55137]

Jews assembled for deportation wait on the platform in the railway station for further transport. [Photograph #55136]

CONCENTRATION CAMPS

View of a sign outside of Buchenwald which reads: "To the Buchenwald Zoological Park!" [Photograph #42734]

Postwar aerial view of Buchenwald concentration camps, showing the barracks. The lender's handwritten caption reads, "Air photo of concentration camp Buchenwald." [Photograph #42923]

A group of SS officers tour the Hinzert concentration camp. [Photograph #34561]

German civilians remove the bodies of former prisoners at the Ebensee concentration camp. [Photograph #48972]

Three men draped in tallitot lead prayers at the dedication of a memorial at the site of the Pocking concentration camp. [Photograph #44843]

Dedication of a memorial at the site of the Pocking concentration camp. [Photograph #44842]

Dedication of a memorial at the site of the Pocking concentration camp. [Photograph #44841]

The American flag flying at half mast in Buchenwald. [Photograph #23060]

A contemporary photo of the crematorium at Stutthof. [Photograph #12205]

Survivors leaving Ebensee. [Photograph #10228]

Survivors in Woebbelin wait to be evacuated to an American field hospital for medical attention. [Photograph #09278]

Survivors in Woebbelin board trucks for evacuation from the camp to an American field hospital for medical attention. [Photograph #09256]

Women survivors in the Woebbelin concentration camp. [Photograph #09245]

David Rousset, a former correspondent for *Time* and *Life* magazines, helps to evacuate starved prisoners from the newly liberated Woebbelin concentration camp. [Photograph #09220]

The quarry in the Flossenbuerg concentration camp. [Photograph #37268]

A section of the Plaszow concentration camp. [Photograph #03407]

An American soldier inspects a metal press found in Ploemnitz ("Leau" after 10 October 1944), a sub-camp of Buchenwald. [Photograph #01980]

View of corpses exhumed from mass graves in Ploemnitz ("Leau" after 10 October 1944), a sub-camp of Buchenwald. [Photograph #01981]

A group of SS officers converse outside at a construction site in the Hinzert concentration camp. [Photograph #34560]

View of two ovens of the crematorium at the Stutthof concentration camp after the liberation. [Photograph #12199]

View of the former Kaiserwald concentration camp. [Photograph #96897]

An aerial photo of the area around the Ebensee concentration camp. [oversized print]. [Photograph #04164]

View of the Russian camp in one of the Linz sub-camps of Mauthausen. [Photograph #07730]

View of the Melk concentration camp. [Photograph #50532]

Aerial photograph of the Mauthausen sub-camp of Gusen. [Oversized Photo]. [Photograph #04147]

A Soviet honor guard stands next to the stone "stairs of death" (Todesstiege) in the Wiener Graben quarry at the Mauthausen concentration camp. [Photograph #45016]

A sign posted (probably in Buchenwald) that says, "Form the Antinazifront! Remember the Millions of victims Murdered by the Nazis / DEATH TO THE NAZI CRIMINALS." [Photograph #43597]

View of piles of clothing and other remains outside a barracks in the brickyard of Jasenovac III, known as KRPARA. The photograph was taken during the May 1945 inspection of Jasenovac by the State Commission for the Investigation of Crimes Committed by the Occupiers and their Collaborators. [Photograph #46472]

Scale model of the Beaune-la-Rolande internment camp created by Aba Sztern and another inmate. [Photograph #46160]

Survivors and military personnel in Ebensee attend a funeral ceremony at the edge of a mass grave holding some 1500–2000 bodies. [Photograph #10368]

An aerial view of the Mauthausen sub-camp of Gusen. [Oversized Photo]. [Photograph #04152]

Two survivors in Woebbelin cook a can of U. S. Army peas over a fire outside one of the barracks. [Photograph #80126]

The bodies of former prisoners are strewn on the ground in a wooded area in the newly liberated Gunskirchen concentration camp. [Photograph #77164]

Enfeebled survivors of the Woebbelin concentration camp await transportation to hospitals for medical attention. [Photograph #23643]

Corpses exhumed from a mass grave in Ploemnitz ("Leau" after 28 October 1944), a sub-camp of Buchenwald. [Photograph #01973]

An aerial view of the Mauthausen area. [Oversized Photo]. [Photograph #04148]

View of the rabbit cages and livestock barns at the Stutthof concentration camp. Several hundred cages were built in the camp in 1940 to support the breeding of rabbits for their fur. [Photograph #51379]

View of the stone "steps of death" (Todesstiege) in the Mauthausen Wiener Graben quarry. [Photograph #00723]

View of the Wiener Graben quarry at the Mauthausen concentration camp. [Photograph #89973]

View of the Ravensbrueck concentration camp. This photograph is from the SS-Propaganda-Album des Frauen-KZ-Ravensbrueck 1940–1941. [Photograph #15010]

Captain Harold Floyd, a member of the Field Information Agency, inspects the pistol range for executions in the Dachau concentration camp. [Photograph #66483]

Prisoners liberated from Mauthausen, many crowded into a wooden bunk, celebrate their liberation by the American 11th Armored Division. [Photograph #65999]

Anti-Nazi posters in German and Polish drawn by freed prisoners hang outside a barrack of the Buchenwald concentration camp. [Photograph #73313]

Three men draped in tallitot lead prayers at the dedication of a memorial and reburial at the site of the Pocking concentration camp. [Photograph #44844]

View of a tree in the Dachau concentration camp, located near the crematorium, where prisoners were hanged. A sign in four languages identifying how it was used is posted on the tree. [Photograph #80721]

Slovakian personnel in the Novaky labor camp. [Photograph #40067]

View of the former Kaiserwald concentration camp. [Photograph #96898]

View of the former Kaiserwald concentration camp. [Photograph #96896]

Inside page of the June 1, 1945, Mediterranean Edition of "Yank: The Army Weekly," featuring an article on German atrocities at the Buchenwald concentration camp and the Ohrdruf sub-camp. [Photograph #35560A]

A view of the Neuengamme concentration camp. On the left is the camp brick factory. [Photograph #06024]

An aerial photograph of the Dachau concentration camp. [oversize print]. [Photograph #06737]

Majola, the mistress of commandant Amon Goeth, stands on the balcony of his villa in the Plaszow concentration camp with his dog Ralf. [Photograph #05287]

An entrance gate in Plaszow, perhaps to the SS section. [Photograph #03393]

View of the gas chambers at Majdanek after the liberation. [Photograph #04864]

UNIFORMS

The striped skirt of a prison uniform worn at the Auschwitz concentration camp. [Photograph #N00077]

Studio portrait of Buchenwald survivor wearing a prisoner uniform. [Photograph #29049]

The cap of a prison uniform and a number patch worn by concentration camp prisoner Karel Bruml at Auschwitz and Nordhausen. [Photograph #N00048]

Portrait of Agnes Laszlo in her camp uniform taken shortly after liberation. [Photograph #61033]

Studio portrait of Buchenwald survivor Zelig wearing a prisoner uniform. [Photograph #29026]

Detail of prisoners' uniforms displayed on the second floor of the permanent exhibit at the U.S. Holocaust Memorial Museum. [Photograph #N02489]

Aleksander Kulisiewicz, dressed in a concentration camp uniform, performs "Muselman" at the Theater Communale in Bologna, Italy. [Photograph #45829]

Portrait of Joseph Schleifstein wearing his old Buchenwald uniform. [Photograph #85913]

Prisoners' clothing and uniforms hang outside the crematorium in the newly liberated Dachau concentration camp. [Photograph #62251]

Portrait of the donor, Alexander Feuer, in his former concentration camp uniform. [Photograph #02109]

Studio portrait of David Bajer wearing the jacket of his concentration camp uniform, taken shortly after his liberation. [Photograph #45509]

A pile of uniforms with distinctive badges discovered in the Breendonck concentration camp. [Photograph #12233]

Aleksander Kulisiewicz, dressed in a concentration camp uniform, performs the "Choral, from the Depths of Hell" at the Theater Communale in Bologna, Italy. [Photograph #45828]

A child survivor in a uniform stands smiling amid the rubble of Nordhausen concentration camp. [Photograph #42050]

The striped overcoat of a prison uniform worn at the Buchenwald concentration camp bearing a purple triangle on the number patch. [Photograph #N00268]

A large group of young Serbian children from the Kozara region who are dressed in Ustasa uniform are assembled at the Stara Gradiska concentration camp. [Photograph #46587]

Portrait of a member of the Buchenwald children's transport wearing his camp uniform. [Photograph #38342]

View of a huge pile of prisoner uniforms in front of a row of barracks in the newly liberated Dachau concentration camp. [Photograph #62246]

Portrait of Pal Kornhauser in the uniform of a captain in the Hungarian army. [Photograph #14676]

Display of concentration camp prisoner uniforms in the permanent exhibition of the U.S. Holocaust Memorial Museum. [Photograph #N02490]

Jewish women press Nazi military uniforms in a workshop in the Glubokoye ghetto. [Photograph #08057]

Joseph Schleifstein, wearing his old Buchenwald uniform, is interviewed by a journalist. [Photograph #07230]

Portrait of Miroslav Filipovic-Majstorovic in Ustasa uniform. [Photograph #37690]

Studio portrait of Buchenwald survivor, Ludwig Grunberger, wearing a prisoner uniform. [Photograph #29093]

Studio portrait of Buchenwald survivor, Benek, wearing a prisoner uniform. [Photograph #29058]

View of the door to the gas chamber at Dachau next to a large pile of uniforms. [Photograph #31327]

Studio portrait of Buchenwald survivor, Heniek Kaliksztajn, wearing a prisoner uniform. [Photograph #28966]

Portrait of an Hungarian Jew dressed in the uniform of the Arrow Cross. [Photograph #94470]

Portrait of Joseph Schleifstein wearing his concentration camp uniform a year or two after his liberation. [Photograph #09557]

Portrait of the donor's uncle, Shmuel Kaplan, in military uniform. [Photograph #21665]

Portrait of Albert Levy in his scout uniform. [Photograph #49490]

Studio portrait of Avraham Gurshofski in his Polish army uniform. [Photograph #39370]

Survivors from an unidentified concentration camp, most of whom are still in uniform, pose for a group photograph. [Photograph #24896]

Dressed in his former concentration camp uniform, the Jewish DP child Joseph Schleifstein attends a memorial service in Buchenwald. [Photograph #09558]

Portrait of Sigmund Gotthelf in German Army uniform during the First World War. [Photograph #30919]

A group of young Serbian children from the Kozara region who are dressed in Ustasa uniform are assembled next to a bus in the Stara Gradiska concentration camp. [Photograph #46580]

A German soldier with an accordian performs together with a guitarist who is not in uniform. [Photograph #43110]

Alexander Markon in French military uniform. [Photograph #40057]

Szaja Ajzen walks along a street in Chelm in military uniform. [Photograph #25509]

Two men wearing striped prisoner uniforms stand next to a monument memorializing Jewish transports that passed through Eisenerz. [Photograph #96438]

Portrait of a Jewish boy dressed in his school uniform. [Photograph #23372]

Portrait of Yaakov Shapira in his British uniform. [Photograph #97186]

Portrait of Bernhard Diament in the uniform of the Danish Navy. [Photograph #59705]

Two insignia from the uniform of the Vichy fascist youth movement, Moisson Nouvelles. [Photograph #24793]

Students at the Rabbinical College in Rhodes in uniform. [Photograph #49413]

Uniformed Nazis congregate along a street in Nuremberg that is bedecked with Nazi banners (probably in celebration of the Reichsparteitag [Reich Party Day] of 1937). [Photograph #64448]

Close-up portrait of Albert Farhi on a street in Sofia wearing his volunteer service uniform. [Photograph #42468]

Portrait of Imre Rosner dressed in the uniform of the Hungarian labor service. [Photograph #27417]

A recent immigrant walks down a street in Tel Aviv in his army uniform. [Photograph #67752]

Portrait of Israel Diament in the uniform of the Danish Brigade in Sweden. [Photograph #59717]

Shmuel Shalkovsky poses between his parents in his Hashomer Hatzair uniform. [Photograph #49389]

Portrait of Bernhard Diament in the uniform of the Danish Brigade. [Photograph #59709]

Three Buchenwald survivors pose on the grass in their uniforms after liberation. [Photograph #18557]

Group portrait of six Macedonian Jewish men, one of whom is wearing military uniform. [Photograph #57927]

Group portrait of young Macedonian Jewish men, many of whom are wearing military uniform. [Photograph #57926]

Portrait of five young survivors of the Buchenwald concentration camp in their uniforms. [Photograph #18561]

Portrait of a Macedonian Jew in military uniform. [Photograph #97821]

Zionist youth, many in uniform, stand in formation and sing Hebrew songs. [Photograph #71389]

Group portrait of young Jewish men, some in police uniform, in the Zeilsheim displaced person's camp. [Photograph #66217]

Studio portrait of Leon Tec wearing his high school uniform. [Photograph #43992]

Reichsfuehrer-SS Heinrich Himmler poses outside in uniform with his hands on his hips. [Photograph #60424]

Portrait of a Jewish nurse, Anya Pevsner, in her uniform. [Photograph #60317]

Felicja Berland poses with her friend Genia Laks wearing the hats of their school uniform. [Photograph #83369]

Serbian boys dressed in Ustasa uniforms are assembled in the Stara Gradiska concentration camp. [Photograph #46555]

Close-up portrait of a teenager wearing his Maccabi Hatzair uniform. [Photograph #71396]

Seven-year-old Shmuel Rabinovitch wearing his school uniform from the Schwabe Hebrew Gymnasium. [Photograph #18313]

Portrait of Marion van Binsbergen Pritchard in her UNRRA uniform. [Photograph #89827]

Jews at forced labor sewing military uniforms for the German army and air force at a factory in the Olkusz ghetto. [Photograph #10032]

Portrait of Sandor Guttman in the uniform of a Hungarian labor battalion with his arm in a sling. [Photograph #26723]

Children, some of whom are dressed in Ustasa uniforms, stand outside a barracks in the Gornja Rijeka concentration camp. [Photograph #46563]

Mosa (Moshe) Mandil poses in army uniform with his parents, Regina and David Mandil. [Photograph #25104]

SHOES

Workers manufacture wooden shoes in the Lodz ghetto. [Photograph #95190A]

Jewish workers manufacture wooden shoes in a workshop in the Lodz ghetto. [Photograph #65816]

Workers stack wooden soles in a large pile in the Lodz ghetto wooden shoe factory. [Photograph #95191A]

Three men walk past the entrance to the straw shoe workshop in the Lodz ghetto. [Photograph #65817]

Children try on shoes in the Jewish owned Erlanger shoe and dry goods store in Guntersblum, Germany. [Photograph #44874]

Huge pile of shoes collected in the Pabianice labor camp/storage facility. [Photograph #65811]

Workers sort coils of straw in the factory for straw shoes of the Lodz ghetto. [Photograph #95199A]

Workers roll up coils of straw in the straw shoe factory of the Lodz ghetto. [Photograph #95198B]

Workers roll up coils of straw in the straw shoe factory of the Lodz ghetto. [Photograph #95198A]

Women twist straw into rope in the courtyard of the straw shoe factory in the Lodz ghetto. [Photograph #95197A]

Workers pile coils of straw onto a horse-drawn cart outside the factory for straw shoes in the Lodz ghetto. [Photograph #95196A]

Jewish women at work producing house shoes in the Glubokoye ghetto. [Photograph #07980]

Jewish men at work producing wooden shoes in the Glubokoye ghetto. [Photograph #07973]

Prisoners labor in a shoe-making workshop in the Jasenovac III concentration camp. [Photograph #46622]

A pair of shoes left behind after a deportation action in the Kovno ghetto. [Photograph #81082]

View of a large pile of victims' shoes piled up outside barracks in the Dachau concentration camp. [Photograph #75004]

A train filled with coils of straw for the shoe factory travels through a street of the Lodz ghetto. [Photograph #65790]

The shoes of prisoners killed at the Gradina execution site near the Jasenovac concentration camp. [Photograph #46552]

Rivesaltes children wearing their new shoes. [Photograph #30077]

Jews at work in a shoe factory in the Szarkowszczyzna ghetto. [Photograph #78937]

Children at the Rivesaltes internment camp receive new shoes. [Photograph #30073]

Cobblers make shoes in the Neu Freimann displaced persons camp. [Photograph #29310]

A young man prepares a wooden sole in a shoe-making workshop in the Warsaw ghetto. [Photograph #45071]

A group of girls pose for a photograph, wearing shoes made at the camp. [Photograph #62430]

An elderly, religious Jewish vendor offers old shoes and boots for sale at an outdoor market in the Warsaw ghetto. [Photograph #15988]

Jewish men at work in a shoemaking workshop. [Photograph #74529A]

Vendors sell old shoes and other items of used clothing at an open air market in the Warsaw ghetto. [Photograph #16004]

Composite photograph of items of apparel used by female members of a German Sinti (Gypsy) tribe, including two skirts, a blouse, a purse and a pair of shoes. [Photograph #N00506]

Women weave shoes and other decorations of raffia at the Rivesaltes internment camp. [Photograph #62432]

A pair of red wooden clogs similar to those worn by most residents of Le Chambon-sur-Lignon, France, as the war wore on and shoes became harder to come by. [Photograph #N00736.36]

Children stand in line to exchange their old shoes for new ones at the Rivesaltes internment camp. [Photograph #30074]

A display of confiscated valuables, some buried in the heels of shoes, collected and sorted in the Pabianice labor camp/storage facility. [Photograph #95265A]

A display of confiscated valuables, some buried in the heels of shoes, collected and sorted in the Pabianice labor camp/storage facility. [Photograph #95264A]

Survivors of Bergen-Belsen walk along the main street of the camp, past a pile of victims' shoes. [Photograph #75113]

Auschwitz women inmates sort through a huge pile of shoes from the transport of Hungarian Jews. [Photograph #77394]

A group of girls pose for a photograph, wearing shoes made at the camp. [Photograph #62431]

View of the Kertesz shoe store in Kosice, Slovakia, owned by the Jewish businessman, Samuel Kertesz. [Photograph #16726]

Jewish women make shoe polish at a workshop in the Glubokoye ghetto. [Photograph #08086]

Six children pose for a photograph at the Rivesaltes internment camp, some of whom wear shoes provided by the aid workers. [Photograph #62435]

A warehouse full of shoes and clothing confiscated from the prisoners and deportees gassed upon their arrival. [Photograph #15330]

Sandals and shoes woven of raffia at the Rivesaltes internment camp. [Photograph #62433]

A pair of boots worn by a female Jewish prisoner in the Plaszow and Auschwitz concentration camps, as well as on a death march. [Photograph #N08521]

Damaged photograph of Dov Levin, a Jewish school boy in pre-war Kovno, that was preserved through the war by a friend in the sole of her shoe. [Photograph #88943]

Tonia Lechtman dsitributes clothing and shoes to Jewish orphans on behalf of UNRRA at an unidentified children's home after the war. [Photograph #25406]

Leo Fraenkel poses with his nieces and nephew in the Erlanger shoe and dry goods store in Guntersblum, Germany. [Photograph #44877]

A note signed by Nazi physician Herta Oberhauser stating that the Polish political prisoner Jadwiga Dzido, who was subjected to medical experiments on her leg, should wear shoes and stockings. [Photograph #63561]

UNRRA workers distribute clothes and shoes to children awaiting on a field. [Photograph #21325]

Portrait of Israel Rakowski that his mother kept hidden in her shoe during her imprisonment in labor and concentration camps. [Photograph #42604]

Portrait of Shmuel Rakowski that his mother kept hidden in her shoe during her imprisonment in labor and concentration camps. [Photograph #42603]

Cobblers making boots in the Neu Freimann displaced persons camp. [Photograph #29351]

Women sew cloth slippers in one of the workshops in the Lodz ghetto. [Photograph #23557]

A sign in Polish from the Belzec killing center that reads, "Attention! All belongings must be handed in at the counter except for money, documents and other valuables, which you must keep with you." [Photograph #46761]

Portrait of Siegfried and Selma Meyer Cohn (the inlaws of the donor) in their garden in Koblenz. [Photograph #18272]

A diploma from International Refugee Organization (IRO) certifying that Naftali Froimowicz is trained as a shoemaker. [Photograph #96472]

Photograph of children's feet clad in ragged sandals. [Photograph #62428]

A young Polish cobbler looks out his window in Poland. [Photograph #47290]

Jewish men at work in a shoemaking workshop in the Glubokoye ghetto. [Photograph #07968]

A view of a child's feet clad in ragged sandals. [Photograph #62427]

A cobbler works at the entrance to his shop in one of the camps on Cyprus. [Photograph #27133]

Jewish youth at work in a shoemaking workshop in the Glubokoye ghetto. [Photograph #07957]

The feet of two men who are standing on a street in the Kovno Ghetto. [Photograph #25152]

Jewish artisans work in a small shoemaking workshop in Krakow shortly before entering the ghetto. [Photograph #74949]

Jewish men and women make felt boots in a workshop in the Glubokoye ghetto. [Photograph #08014]

Jewish men and women make felt boots in a workshop in the Glubokoye ghetto. [Photograph #07988]

A destitute man and child sit against a wall on a street in the Warsaw ghetto. [Photograph #69958]

A barefoot woman and a young man in the doorway of a shoemaker's shop in the Warsaw ghetto. [Photograph #11913]

Portrait of Berisz Putersznyt sent to his daughter who was in the Oberalstadt concentration camp. [Photograph #27094]

A member of the French resistance sorts through a warehouse filled with discarded prisoners' clothing in the Natzweiler-Struthof concentration camp. [Photograph #02018]

At the main gate to the Krzemieniec ghetto, Jewish children polish the boots of Jewish policemen as German soldiers look on. [Photograph #09525]

A painting by artist Sophia Kalski depicting Lwow in February 1943. [Photograph #N10934]

Jewish youth learn shoemaking in a workshop in either the Foehrenwald or Windsheim displaced persons' camp. [Photograph #34853]

Greeting card given to Jadwiga Hassa by Jadwiga Solecka, a fellow inmate of the Ravensbrueck concentration camp. [Photograph #63559]

Portrait of Natalia Netka Putersznyt sent to her daughter who was in the Oberalstadt concentration camp. [Photograph #27093]

Street scene in the Warsaw ghetto. [Photograph #69971]

Bare-footed German women from Nammering look at the corpses of prisoners exhumed from a mass grave near the town. [Photograph #04479]

Bare-footed German women are forced by American soldiers to walk among the corpses of prisoners exhumed from a mass grave near Nammering. [Photograph #04482]

JEWELRY

Jewelry boxes made by prisoners at a Slovakian labor camp. [Photograph #72027]

A female vendor offers jewelry, used clothing, and other items for sale on the street in the Warsaw ghetto. [Photograph #07528]

Metal brooch designed in imitation of the ration card issued to Bela Bialer in the Lodz ghetto. [Photograph #N02815]

An Omega watch belonging to Bela Gondos, a physician who was a passenger on the Kasztner rescue train. [Photograph #N09727]

Star of David beaded necklace made by a female Jewish prisoner at a munitions factory camp in Germany. [Photograph #N06164]

Confiscated jewels. [Photograph #95134A]

Abba P. Schwartz, property control director for the Intergovernmental Committee on Refugees (left), and Col. William G. Brey, chief of the Foreign Exchange Depository (right), view a crate of gold and silver jewelry confiscated by the Germans during World War II. [Photograph #73024]

U.S. Army Signal Corps pin issued to combat photographer Arnold E. Samuelson. [Photograph #N00181]

Two small metal crucifixes worn by Charles Weingarten and his mother, Margarethe, while they were living in hiding in Nice during the German occupation. [Photograph #N09150]

Jewish workers assemble watches in a workshop in Poland. [Photograph #59818]

Silver pin from the Schlachtensee displaced persons camp, with the Hebrew inscription "Speak Hebrew." [Photograph #N05787]

A Jewish prisoner is forced to remove his ring upon his arrival in the Jasenovac concentration camp. [Photograph #68290]

Rosary beads with a pendant crucifix given to the Jewish child, Lida Kleinman, while she was living in hiding in Poland during the German occupation. [Photograph #N09149]

Oval Betar Zionist youth movement stickpin with the image of a menorah and the designation "Betar," in Hebrew. [Photograph #N05788]

Rectangular Betar Zionist youth movement pin with the raised profile of founder Vladimir Jabotinsky (1880-1940). [Photograph #N05789]

A display of boxes of gold caps and dentures removed from prisoners in Buchenwald and recovered by American troops after the liberation of the concentration camp. [Photograph #74565]

Rosary beads given to Irena Schwarz, a Jewish child living in hiding in occupied Poland, by her rescuer Janina Sycz. [Photograph #N09442]

Detail of the "In the Camps" photo mural and brooch displayed on the third floor of the permanent exhibition at the U.S. Holocaust Memorial Museum. [Photograph #N02453]

A display of confiscated valuables, some buried in the heels of shoes, collected and sorted in the Pabianice labor camp/storage facility. [Photograph #95264A]

A watch given to Anna Cheszes by her rescuer Madzia Strzelczyk. [Photograph #N09430]

An American soldier views an array of stones and other valuables confiscated from prisoners in the Buchenwald concentration camp and recovered by U.S. troops after the liberation of the camp. [Photograph #73025]

A soldier dips his hands into a crate full of rings confiscated from prisoners in Buchenwald and found by American troops in a cave adjoining the concentration camp. [Photograph #80623]

Marc Jarblum addresses a crowd of DPs at a demonstration protesting the forced return of the Exodus 1947 passengers to Europe. [Photograph #11513]

HAIR

Bales of the hair of female prisoners found in the warehouses of Auschwitz at the liberation. [Photograph #85742]

Bales of hair from female prisoners, numbered for shipment to Germany, found at the liberation of Auschwitz. [Photograph #14220]

Bales of human hair ready for shipment to Germany found in one of the Auschwitz warehouses when the camp was liberated. In Auschwitz 7,000 kilos of human hair were found at liberation. [Photograph #66583]

Bales containing the hair of female prisoners lie in the courtyard of one of the warehouses in Auschwitz after the liberation. [Photograph #10867]

Members of the French resistance shear the hair of a young woman who consorted with the Germans during the occupation. [Photograph #81863]

Nadia Cohen (with short hair) with the children that she is taking care of in the camp. [Photograph #44542]

Nadia Cohen with a group in Israel that came on Aliyah. Nadiah is on the right (with short black hair) behind three kids. [Photograph #44537]

A large group of adults and children gathers together inside a room in the Lodz ghetto. Among those pictured is Ruth Berlinska (front wearing a bow in her hair). [Photograph #21402]

A young Jewish girl in hiding with dyed blond hair walks in a field of tall grass. Pictured is Krystyna Lindenbaum. [Photograph #16068]

Young girls, dressed in overalls and with flowers in their hair, put on a school performance at the Novaky labor camp. Among those pictured are Mira Frenkel (third from right) and twin sisters (first and second from the right). [Photograph #72066]

Jewish women learn to sew in a vocational training workshop in Lodz. The woman in the back has her head fully covered since her hair still has not grown in since the war. [Photograph #60791]

A eugenics chart entitled: "Hereditary traits passed down from two mates. Simplified portrayal [of hereditary traits] given the assumption of only one pair of mates both for eye color and hair type." [Photograph #N09514]

ZYKLON B CANISTERS

Labels taken from canisters of Zyklon B from the Dachau Gas Installation. The first and third panels contain the German Pest Control Company emblem and the brand name Zyklon. [Photograph #03563]

A canister of Zyklon B found in the Dachau concentration camp and clearly marked as poison with a skull and crossbones. [Photograph #75047]

GAS CHAMBERS

The door to the gas chamber in Dachau. It is marked "shower-bath."
[Photograph #00276]

Interior view of a gas chamber in the Mauthausen concentration camp. Original text reads: "This is the gas chamber, note how it looks like a shower room. Camp Mauthausen." [Photograph #23839]

Interior view of the gas chamber in the Dachau concentration camp.
[Photograph #75045]

View of the door to the gas chamber in the Dachau concentration camp. A sign above it identifies it as a shower. [Photograph #75046]

View of the door to the gas chamber at Dachau next to a large pile of uniforms.
[Photograph #31327]

A door to a gas chamber in Auschwitz. The note reads: Harmful gas! Entering endangers your life. [Photograph #14614]

View a medical table used for removing gold teeth from prisoners at the Mauthausen concentration camp. Original caption reads: "This is the chamber where they knocked out gold teeth, after they were gassed by SS men." [Photograph #23836]

Detail of the scale model of crematorium II at Auschwitz-Birkenau on display in the permanent exhibition of the U. S. Holocaust Memorial Museum. The model was sculpted by Mieczyslaw Stobierski based on contemporary documents and the trial testimonies of SS guards. [Photograph #N00479]

A soldier from the U. S. 7th Army examines the door to a gas chamber in the Dachau concentration camp. [Photograph #61985]

A canister of Zyklon B found in the Dachau concentration camp and clearly marked as poison with a skull and crossbones. [Photograph #75047]

A contemporary view of the gas chambers at Stutthof. [Photograph #12206]

View of the walled entrance to the gas chamber in the main camp of Auschwitz (Auschwitz I). This gas chamber was in use for only a short time before being converted into a bomb shelter. [Photograph #50773]

Crematorium furnaces in the Gusen concentration camp after the liberation. [Photograph #06435]

View of the gas chambers at Majdanek after the liberation. [Photograph #04864]

British soldiers walk past a cremation oven after the destruction and liberation of Bergen-Belsen. [Photograph #44595]

Close-up view of an oven in the crematoria of the Dachau concentration camp filled with human remains. [Photograph #33752]

American soldiers walk past the crematorium in the Dachau concentration camp. [Photograph #75049]

View of a cremation oven in the Dachau concentration camp. [Photograph #75048]

Two men stand in front of a stack of coffins in the newly liberated Dachau concentration camp holding urns of ashes. [Photograph #69458]

View of one of the ovens in the crematorium at the Ebensee concentration camp. [Photograph #48973]

An American soldier inspects the crematorium in Buchenwald. [Photograph #82224]

A survivor stokes smoldering human remains in a crematorium oven that is still lit. [Photograph #00315]

American soldiers view a pile of human remains outside the crematorium in Buchenwald. [Photograph #20308]

Ruins of crematorium II. [Photograph #08857]

An American soldier tests the crematorium elevator while on an inspection of the Natzweiler-Struthof concentration camp. [Photograph #02005]

The new crematorium in Dachau, which was completed in May 1944. [Photograph #05810]

Two ovens inside the crematorium at the Dachau concentration camp. [Photograph #80722]

Crematoria ovens in Buchenwald concentration camp. [Photograph #80255]

The charred remains of former prisoners in two crematoria ovens in the newly liberated Buchenwald concentration camp. [Photograph #80253]

View of crematorium ovens at the Majdanek concentration camp after the liberation. [Photograph #05548]

A crematoria oven in Ebensee, a sub-camp of Mauthausen. [Photograph #04880]

Corpses laid out for cremation in the Mauthausen concentration camp. [Photograph #01993]

Survivors in Mauthausen open one of the crematoria ovens for American troops who are inspecting the camp. [Photograph #77019]

Human remains found by American troops in the crematoria ovens of Buchenwald. [Photograph #82856]

Close-up view of a cremation oven after the destruction and liberation of Bergen-Belsen. The original caption states, "Cremator, where they burned the people who were sick." [Photograph #44596]

A British sergeant inspects a cremation oven after the liberation of Bergen-Belsen. The original caption states, "Sgt Waxer looks at the cremator in Belsen." [Photograph #44594]

Trapdoor inside the crematorium at Buchenwald concentration camp. Original Caption Reads: "Trap door to basement of crematorium through which victims were thrown." [Photograph #48908]

Human remains of prisoners found near the crematorium at the Dachau concentration camp. Original caption reads: "Bone pile outside the crematory at the Dachau concentration camp." [Photograph #49658]

Interior view of a circular room known as the "Gas Chamber" which was used as a mortuary. [Photograph #11887]

Interior view of a circular room known as the "Gas Chamber" which was used as a mortuary. [Photograph #11852]

Prisoners' clothing and uniforms hang outside the crematorium in the newly liberated Dachau concentration camp. [Photograph #62251]

Partial view of the crematorium, focusing on the chimney, in the newly liberated Dachau concentration camp. [Photograph #62239]

Prisoners' clothing and uniforms are piled in front of the doors to the crematoria in the newly liberated Dachau concentration camp. [Photograph #62236]

Partial view of the crematorium in the newly liberated Dachau concentration camp. [Photograph #62234]

Trucks are parked in front of the crematorium in the newly liberated Dachau concentration camp. [Photograph #62223]

An aerial reconnaissance photograph showing Auschwitz-Birkenau. [Photograph #05365]

Survivors of the Dachau concentration camp prepare to move a corpse during a demonstration of the cremation process at the camp. [Photograph #15029A]

Members of an international commission of inquiry view the ruins of the crematorium in Auschwitz-Birkenau. [Photograph #10873]

A member of an international commission of inquiry views the ruins of one of the crematoria in Auschwitz-Birkenau. [Photograph #10871]

Jewish women and children from Subcarpathian Rus who have been selected for death at Auschwitz-Birkenau, walk toward the gas chambers. The building in the background is crematorium III. [Photograph #77346]

Jewish women and children who have been selected for death, walk in a line towards the gas chambers. The gate at the upper left leads to the section of the camp on the south side of the ramp known as BI. [Photograph #77298]

MASS GRAVES

A corpse slides down a shoot into a mass grave in the Warsaw ghetto. [Photograph #05530]

View of a mass grave pictured after the liberation of Bergen-Belsen. [Photograph #44589]

View of a mass grave pictured in Bergen-Belsen after liberation. [Photograph #44590]

Jewish survivors watch as Poles exhume a mass grave in Sokolow Podlaski. [Photograph #15077]

View of a mass grave pictured after the liberation of Bergen-Belsen. The original caption states, "Graves that had been dug up to bury the prisoners as they died." [Photograph #44591]

Laborers at the Jewish cemetery on Okopowa Street bury bodies in a mass grave. Joest's original caption reads: "Then he let the corpses slide over the edge down into the pit to the man below, who stacked them next to each other." [Photograph #69998]

View of a large mass grave in the Warsaw ghetto cemetery. Joest's original caption reads: "Next to the mass graves in which hundreds of corpses had been laid, a new one had already been dug." [Photograph #69969]

An undertaker views a layer of corpses laid out at the bottom of a mass grave in the Okopowa Street cemetery. Joest's caption reads: "Once again a layer of the dead was finished and now had to be covered with lime." [Photograph #32165]

The mass grave near Nammering from which the bodies of prisoners shot by the SS were exhumed following the occupation of the area by U. S. troops. [Photograph #04481]

Three men peer into a large mass grave filled with the naked corpses (probably of victims from Dachau). [Photograph #33750]

A laborer at the Jewish cemetery on Okopowa Street buries bodies in a mass grave. Joest's original caption reads: "The man down below stood on the lime. He had to place the corpses as close together as possible to save space." [Photograph #69999]

Makeshift tombstones mark the mass grave of Jewish victims in the Warsaw ghetto. [Photograph #73014A]

Two American officers with the 94th Division count the bodies of 71 political prisoners exhumed from a mass grave on Wenzelnberg near Solingen-Ohligs. The victims, most of whom were taken from Luettringhausen prison, were shot and buried by the Gestapo following orders to eliminate all Reich enemies just before the end of the war. [Photograph #08184]

Survivors and military personnel in Ebensee attend a funeral ceremony at the edge of a mass grave holding some 1500-2000 bodies. [Photograph #10368]

A memorial wreath on the site of a mass grave in the Ebensee concentration camp. [Photograph #06549]

Residents of the Warsaw ghetto attend a funeral in the ghetto cemetery. In the foreground is a mass grave that has just been covered over. Joest's original caption reads: "This huge grave pit had just been covered over." [Photograph #69983]

A boy working in the Warsaw ghetto cemetery drags a corpse to the edge of the mass grave where it will be buried. Joest's caption reads: "The boy slid the dead over the edge into the pit." [Photograph #32168]

The local Burgomeister views the partially exhumed mass grave in Stamsried, Germany. (Photograph taken by the 166th Signal Corps Company.) [Photograph #41612]

Close-up of Ustasa victims lying in a mass grave. [Photograph #46461]

Liberated prisoners bury those who died on the Schwandorf death train. [Photograph #42593]

American soldiers stand guard along the perimeter of an open mass grave at Mauthausen. [Photograph #04767A]

A partially filled mass grave lies in the foreground as American soldiers walk around a barn outside of Gardelegen in which over 1,000 prisoners were burned alive by the SS. [Photograph #77451]

Under the supervision of American soldiers, German civilians exhume the bodies of 71 political prisoners from a mass grave on Wenzelnberg near Solingen-Ohligs. [Photograph #08174]

Austrian civilians prepare a mass grave to bury former inmates at the Mauthausen concentration camp. [Photograph #15548]

The bodies of former inmates are laid out in a mass grave in the Mauthausen concentration camp. [Photograph #15675]

The bodies of former inmates are laid out in a mass grave in the Mauthausen concentration camp. [Photograph #15674]

View of a mass grave dug by Austrian civilians to bury former inmates in the Mauthausen concentration camp. [Photograph #15631]

Austrian civilians prepare mass graves to bury former inmates in the Mauthausen concentration camp. [Photograph #12763]

An American Army chaplain recites prayers at an open mass grave in the Gusen concentration camp. [Photograph #11458]

Prisoners' bodies laid out in a mass grave. [Photograph #06362]

The bodies of former concentration camp inmates are laid out in a mass grave at Mauthausen. [Photograph #07467]

Survivors place a wreath at the site of a mass grave in the Ebensee concentration camp. [Photograph #80742]

A memorial wreath on the site of a mass grave in the Ebensee concentration camp. [Photograph #06557]

The bodies of former prisoners are laid out in a mass grave at Mauthausen. [Photograph #04767]

German civilians exhume the corpses of Italians shot and buried in shell holes on the orders of the Gestapo in Wilhelmshoehe on March 31, 1945. [Photograph #01959]

View of the north side of the barn outside of Gardelegen. In the foreground are two mass graves in which prisoners who were burned alive were buried by the SS. [Photograph #89081]

View of a mass grave in the Ohrdruf concentration camp from which 2,000 corpses were removed for proper burial. [Photograph #74266]

A partially filled mass grave lies in the foreground as American soldiers walk around a barn outside of Gardelegen in which over 1,000 prisoners were burned alive by the SS. [Photograph #77450]

German civilians toss the corpses of victims (probably from Dachau) into a large mass grave. [Photograph #33748]

The local Burgomeister views the mass grave in Stamsried, Germany, before it is opened for exhumation. (Photograph taken by the 166th Signal Corps Company.) [Photograph #41613]

German civilians exhume bodies from a mass grave in Stamsried, Germany. (Photograph taken by the 166th Signal Corps Company.) [Photograph #41611]

German civilians exhume bodies from a mass grave in Stamsried, Germany. (Photograph taken by the 166th Signal Corps Company.) [Photograph #41610]

German civilians exhume bodies from a mass grave in Stamsried, Germany. (Photograph taken by the 166th Signal Corps Company.) [Photograph #41609]

A group of German civilians stand with their shovels among the corpses of Nazi victims they have just exhumed from a mass grave in Stamsried, Germany. (Photograph taken by the 166th Signal Corps Company.) [Photograph #41606]

The burial ground for the Polish and Soviet infants who died in the nursery in Ruehen. Each of the mounds is a mass grave of infants. [Photograph #96528]

The bodies of former inmates are laid out in a mass grave in the Mauthausen concentration camp. [Photograph #28292]

Under the supervision of American soldiers, German civilians view the bodies of 71 political prisoners from a mass grave on Wenzelnberg near Solingen-Ohligs. The victims, most of whom were taken from Luettringhausen prison, were shot and buried by the Gestapo following orders to eliminate all Reich enemies just before the end of the war. [Photograph #08181]

Under the supervision of an American soldier, German civilians carry the body of one of 71 political prisoners exhumed from a mass grave on Wenzelnberg near Solingen-Ohligs. [Photograph #08177]

Under the supervision of American soldiers, German civilians exhume the bodies of 71 political prisoners from a mass grave on Wenzelnberg near Solingen-Ohligs. [Photograph #08176]

Under the supervision of American soldiers, German civilians exhume the bodies of 71 political prisoners from a mass grave on Wenzelnberg near Solingen-Ohligs. [Photograph #08175]

Handry Hundblut, formerly a major in the SA and wartime tank commandant, exhumes the body of one of 71 political prisoners from a mass grave on Wenzelnberg near Solingen-Ohligs. [Photograph #08173]

German civilians identify the bodies of 71 political prisoners exhumed from a mass grave on Wenzelnberg near Solingen-Ohligs. The victims, most of whom were taken from Luettringhausen prison, were shot and buried by the Gestapo following orders to eliminate all Reich enemies just before the end of the war. [Photograph #08172]

Survivors from Ostrowiec walk toward the site of a mass grave for 2000 Jews shot during the October 1942 action. [Photograph #21086]

Austrian civilians lay the bodies of former inmates in a mass grave in the Mauthausen concentration camp. [Photograph #15547]

Austrian civilians lay the bodies of former inmates in a mass grave in the Mauthausen concentration camp. [Photograph #15546]

The bodies of former inmates are laid out in a mass grave at the Mauthausen concentration camp. [Photograph #11457]

American soldiers in Ludwigslust at the funeral on the palace grounds of the Archduke of Mecklenburg, where the townspeople were forced by U. S. troops to bury the corpses of prisoners killed in the Woebbelin concentration camp. [Photograph #09273]

The bodies of prisoners killed in the Nordhausen concentration camp lie in a mass grave dug by German civilians under orders from American troops. [Photograph #83929]

Austrian civilians dig a mass grave to bury the victims of the Mauthausen concentration camp. [Photograph #04846]

View of corpses exhumed from mass graves in Ploemnitz ("Leau" after 10 October 1944), a sub-camp of Buchenwald. [Photograph #01981]

Under supervision of American soldiers, German civilians exhume the corpses of Italians shot in shell holes on the orders of the Gestapo in Wilhelmshoehe on March 31, 1945. [Photograph #01957]

German civilians exhume the corpses of Italians shot and buried in shell holes on the orders of the Gestapo in Wilhelmshoehe on March 31, 1945. [Photograph #01960]

Austrian civilians prepare a mass grave for the bodies of former inmates at the Gusen concentration camp. [Photograph #68087]

Soviets exhume a mass grave in Zloczow shortly after the liberation. [Photograph #86588]

German prisoners of war from a nearby internment camp are forced to exhume bodies from a mass grave found near the town of Nammering. [Photograph #82999]

German civilians exhume the corpse of a prisoner from a mass grave for proper reburial. [Photograph #82815]

A crowd of people observes the exhumation of a mass grave in the Jewish cemetery of Stanislawow. [Photograph #80762]

German civilians from Schwarzenfeld exhume the bodies of 140 Hungarian, Russian, and Polish Jews from a mass grave near the town. The victims died while on an evacuation transport from the Flossenbuerg concentration camp. [Photograph #79003]

German civilians from Schwarzenfeld exhume the bodies of 140 Hungarian, Russian, and Polish Jews from a mass grave near the town. The victims died while on an evacuation transport from the Flossenbuerg concentration camp. [Photograph #78847]

Under the direction of American soldiers, German civilians bury the bodies of 71 political prisoners, exhumed from a mass grave near Solingen-Ohligs, in new graves in front of the city hall. [Photograph #78815]

Under the direction of American soldiers, German civilians rebury the bodies of 71 political prisoners, exhumed from a mass grave near Solingen-Ohligs, in front of the city hall. [Photograph #78811]

AMERICAN SOLDIERS

German troops surrender to the American 7th Armored Division near Eisborn, Germany. [Photograph #65998]

A Japanese-American soldier with the 522nd Field Artillery battalion poses outside in the snow in Waakirchen, Germany. [Photograph #07726]

Lt. Col. Ralph E. Willey and Lt. Plevinsky pose with Russian soldiers on the steps of the Russian headquarters in Berlin. [Photograph #42049]

Two American soldiers in a jeep drive into Germany from Belgium. To their right is a sign in English that says, "You are entering Germany, an enemy country. Keep on the alert." [Photograph #65997]

American troops pull the survivors of a sunken craft on to the shores of the Normandy beaches. [Photograph #65996]

American troops wade through the surf on their arrival at the Normandy beaches. [Photograph #65995]

Jewish soldiers in the U. S. army hold religious services in a room decorated with Nazi flags. [Photograph #59964]

Cover of the Passover Seder Services brochure issued in March 1945 for American troops from the U. S. Fifth Army. The seder took place at the main railroad station in Florence, Italy. [Photograph #94551]

Japanese-American troops with the 522nd Field Artillery Battalion collect the belongings of three captured German Waffen-SS soldiers. [Photograph #07773]

Chaplain Judah Nadich delivers a sermon to American servicemen at a Thanksgiving service in the rue de la Victoire synagogue in Paris. [Photograph #12632]

An American convoy leads survivors (probably of Buchenwald) out of the camp. [Photograph #43599]

Two American soldiers with their rifles at the ready move away from the scene of a small fire in a town in Germany. [Photograph #66223]

Members of the U. S. 9th Armored Division meet up with units of the Red Army near Linz, Austria. [Photograph #69849]

Members of the U. S. 9th Armored Division meet up with units of the Red Army near Linz, Austria. [Photograph #69848]

Members of the 522nd Field Artillery Battalion in Germany stand in formation with the American and battalion flags. [Photograph #45863]

General Wyman and other American soldiers inspect a death train in Schwandorf, Germany. [Photograph #42590]

U. S. Army troops march through the Brandenburg Gate in Berlin. [Photograph #26308]

German troops who surrendered to Japanese-American troops with the 522nd Field Artillery Battalion receive orders to go home after they have been disarmed. [Photograph #07774]

Liberated prisoners from a Dachau death march stand outside of a barn in Waakirchen, Germany, where Japanese-American soldiers with the 522nd Field Artillery Battalion found them shelter. [Photograph #07745]

Survivors from a death march from Dachau huddle around a camp fire prepared by Japanese-American soldiers with the 522nd Field Artillery Battalion. The soldier on the left is George Oiye. [Photograph #07733]

Japanese-American soldiers with the 522nd Field Artillery Battery catch a ride on a tank near Dachau. [Photograph #07686]

A group of Jewish soldiers in the British army, local Iraqi Jews and Jewish Americans serving in the Air Force and the Army, at a Passover Seder in Baghdad. The Seder was conducted by the British army chaplain, Rabbi Brody. [Photograph #19739]

American soldiers in Dachau examine piles of prisoners' clothing found near the crematorium. [Photograph #19403]

Journalists, accompanied by American military police, conduct an inspection tour of the newly liberated Buchenwald concentration camp. [Photograph #23646]

American soldiers load a piano onto a truck. Original caption: Loading the Loot—a "liberated plane." [Photograph #43121]

Captain Harold Floyd, a member of the Field Information Agency, inspects the pistol range for executions in the Dachau concentration camp. [Photograph #66483]

American soldiers enter a barrack in the Buchenwald concentration camp while a survivor smiles in the foreground. [Photograph #73336]

Liberated prisoners gather by the barbed wire fence in front of stacked wood in an unidentified concentration camp. [Photograph #66705]

American soldiers walk past rows of dead bodies awaiting burial in the Nordhausen concentration camp. [Photograph #64088]

Members of the U. S. 9th Armored Division meet up with units of the Red Army near Linz, Austria. [Photograph #69847]

Members of the U. S. 9th Armored Division meet up with units of the Red Army near Linz, Austria. [Photograph #69846]

Members of the U. S. 9th Armored Division meet up with units of the Red Army near Linz, Austria. [Photograph #69845]

Members of the U. S. 9th Armored Division meet up with units of the Red Army near Linz, Austria. [Photograph #69844]

Members of the U. S. 9th Armored Division meet up with units of the Red Army near Linz, Austria. [Photograph #69841]

Members of the U. S. 9th Armored Division meet up with units of the Red Army near Linz, Austria. [Photograph #69840]

Members of the U. S. 9th Armored Division meet up with units of the Red Army near Linz, Austria. [Photograph #69838]

Japanese-Americans with the 522nd Field Artillery Battalion pose outside the destroyed Berghof, Hitler's mountain retreat in the Bavarian Alps. [Photograph #45864]

Survivors mingle with American soldiers in the newly liberated Dachau concentration camp. [Photograph #62273]

An American soldier poses next to a huge pile of rubble alongside a railroad after the war. [Photograph #57887]

A survivor stands next to a cart filled with corpses in the Hurlach concentration camp. [Photograph #49229]

American troops examine a row of bodies laid out in a row in Hurlach concentration camp. [Photograph #49226]

General Dwight D. Eisenhower on the bridge of a PT boat. [Photograph #37472]

An American soldier inspects the crematorium in Buchenwald. [Photograph #82224]

American troops advance through the streets of Aachen during the liberation of Germany. [Photograph #28278]

American soldiers view the corpses of slave laborers shot by the SS in the vicinity of Hirzenhain. [Photograph #77152]

Survivors in a barracks enjoy bowls of soup given to them by the U. S. Army after the liberation of the Buchenwald concentration camp. [Photograph #12074]

A Japanese-American soldier poses next to his jeep in the town of Waakirchen, where the 522nd Field Artillery Battalion set up a temporary field hospital for survivors of a Dachau death march. [Photograph #07715]

Dachau concentration camp visitor's pass issued July 16, 1945, to Pfc. Neimeister, Lt. Col. Barkin and signed by Lt. Col. A. R. Arend, security officer. [Photograph #04555]

American soldiers view the Dachau death train. [Photograph #19402]

Brigadier General Owen Summers and Colonel Walker look on as Norwegian women suspected of collaborating with the Germans are screened by Allied authorities. [Photograph #81881]

Members of the Dutch resistance, the Dutch police, and an American soldier search for uniforms and weapons belonging to Dutchmen suspected of collaborating with the Germans during the occupation. [Photograph #81880]

Displaced persons in the town of Dillenburg after the liberation of the area by U. S. troops. [Photograph #09583]

Survivors in Woebbelin speaking with their American liberators. [Photograph #09284]

Members of the US army visit the Zeilsheim displaced persons' camp. [Photograph #89683]

Jewish soldiers in the American Army attend High Holiday services on a hillside near the newly established Seventh Corps headquarters in Kornelimünster, near Aachen, Germany. [Photograph #04725]

An American soldier and local civilian official examine corpses found near Warstein. The victims were shot by German police prior to the arrival of U. S. troops. [Photograph #02027]

An American soldier stands among the corpses of prisoners exhumed from a mass grave near Nammering. [Photograph #04473]

An African-American soldier with the 12th Armored Division, Seventh U. S. Army, stands guard over a group of German soldiers captured in the forest. [Photograph #83790]

Slave laborers in the town of Altenkirchen who were liberated by the U. S. First Army collect their belongings and await evacuation to a nearby area. [Photograph #75606]

American and Russian Soldiers assist in the evacuation of the DP camps. Original caption reads: Russian major checking with Gen. Russian Lt. in foreground. [Photograph #48906]

A group of liberating U. S. Army soldiers speaking with prisoners in the Buchenwald concentration camp. Original Caption reads: As we entered the camp former inmates approached us, telling us about the place and offering to serve as guides. [Photograph #48904]

Group of American soldiers congregates in front of a tent displaying a Nazi flag as a door. Original caption reads: Nazi flag makes a good tent flap. Heading above photographs: The 120th set up in suburban Race Track near Frankfurt a/m April 5-15. [Photograph #42733]

American soldiers walk among corpses that are laid out in rows in the Nordhausen concentration camp. [Photograph #29568]

American troops guard a prison for former SS troops on the site of the Dachau concentration camp. [Photograph #66484]

American soldiers walk past the crematorium in the Dachau concentration camp. [Photograph #75049]

Two survivors walk past a barrack in the Buchenwald concentration camp carrying a large cannister (probably containing soup). [Photograph #73324]

A U. S. Army combat photographer with the 167th Signal Corps Company prepares his camera on the back of a truck. [Photograph #62777]

Portrait of a U. S. Army combat photographer wearing a shoulder patch identifying him as an official U. S. war photographer. [Photograph #62775]

General Dwight D. Eisenhower talks to US troops who are marching with their gear alongside a train. [Photograph #64087]

Members of the U. S. 9th Armored Division meet up with units of the Red Army near Linz, Austria. [Photograph #69843]

Members of the U. S. 9th Armored Division meet up with units of the Red Army near Linz, Austria. [Photograph #69839]

Clarence Matsamura, a Japanese-American soldier in the 522nd Field Artillery Battalion in Germany, poses next to a 522 EMS club sign. Matsamura was the soldier who liberated Jewish survivor Solly Ganor from a death march in Waakirchen. [Photograph #45866]

Two Japanese-American soldiers with the 522nd Field Artillery Battalion stand in front of the crematorium in the Dachau concentration camp soon after the liberation. [Photograph #45865]

American troops advance through the streets of Aachen during the liberation of Germany. [Photograph #62858]

LIBERATION

Albanian communist leader, Enver Hoxha (center), reviews the troops at a military parade marking the liberation of Tirana. [Photograph #24735]

Russian, Polish and Jewish prisoners in Dachau celebrate their liberation by American forces. [Photograph #57861]

View of the barracks at Dachau concentration camp. Original caption reads: "Notorious prison camp at Dachau, liberated by the 45th Division, in their drive to Munich." [Photograph #49662]

Human remains of prisoners found near the crematorium at the Dachau concentration camp. Original caption reads: "Bone pile outside the crematory at the Dachau concentration camp." [Photograph #49658]

View of the Kaufering IV concentration camp, a sub-camp of Dachau, taken on the day of liberation. [Photograph #04434]

Mug shot of an S. S. guard (Schulz) stationed at Dachau, who was arrested when the camp was liberated by American forces on April 29, 1945. [Photograph #49687]

Mug shot of an S. S. guard (Kick) stationed at Dachau, who was arrested when the camp was liberated by American forces on April 29, 1945. [Photograph #49686]

Mug shot of an S. S. guard (Wagner) stationed at Dachau, who was arrested when the camp was liberated by American forces on April 29, 1945. [Photograph #49685]

Mug shot of an S. S. guard (Betz) stationed at Dachau, who was arrested when the camp was liberated by American forces on April 29, 1945. [Photograph #49684]

Mug shot of Dachau Camp Commandant from 1942-1943, Martin Gottfried Weiss, who was arrested when the camp was liberated by American forces on April 29, 1945. [Photograph #49682]

Mug shot of an S. S. guard (Moll) stationed at Dachau, who was arrested when the camp was liberated by American forces on April 29, 1945. [Photograph #49681]

Mug shot of Hans Kurt Eisle, a physician stationed at Dachau, who was arrested when the camp was liberated by American forces on April 29, 1945. [Photograph #49679]

Mug shot of an S. S. guard (Froschuer) stationed at Dachau, who was arrested when the camp was liberated by American forces on April 29, 1945. [Photograph #49678]

Mug shot of an S. S. guard (Welter) stationed at Dachau, who was arrested when the camp was liberated by American forces on April 29, 1945. [Photograph #49677]

Mug shot of an S. S. guard (Redwitz) stationed at Dachau, who was arrested when the camp was liberated by American forces on April 29, 1945. [Photograph #49674]

Mug shot of an S. S. guard (Vidermayer) stationed at Dachau, who was arrested when the camp was liberated by American forces on April 29, 1945. [Photograph #49673]

Mug shot of an S. S. guard (Hippmann) stationed at Dachau, who was arrested when the camp was liberated by American forces on April 29, 1945. [Photograph #49672]

Mug shot of an S. S. guard (Suttrop) stationed at Dachau, who was arrested when the camp was liberated by American forces on April 29, 1945. [Photograph #49671]

Mug shot of Dr. Klaus Karl Schilling who performed medical experiments on the prisoners of Dachau, mostly concerning the effects and treatments of Malaria. He was arrested when the camp was liberated by American forces on April 29, 1945. [Photograph #49670]

Mug shot of an S. S. guard (Fileboeck) stationed at Dachau, who was arrested by the Americans when they liberated the camp on April 29, 1945. [Photograph #49668]

Mug shot of an S. S. guard (Wahl) stationed at Dachau, who was arrested when the camp was liberated by American forces on April 29, 1945. [Photograph #49665]

Mug shot of an S. S. guard (Betz) stationed at Dachau, who was arrested when the camp was liberated by American forces on April 29, 1945. [Photograph #49664]

Belgian civilians celebrate the liberation of Brussels with Allied troops. [Photograph #65985]

Romanian citizens surround and greet the first Soviet soldiers to enter Bucharest. [Photograph #61919]

Jacques Grootkerk and members of the Princess Irene Brigade of Dutch Free Forces rides in a military vehicle in the liberation parade in Amsterdam. [Photograph #13038]

General Henning Linden, assistant commanding general, 42nd Rainbow Infantry Division, gives directions to his troops from the parapet of the bridge at the Jourhaus at the entrance to the Dachau concentration camp. [Photograph #08917]

Mug shot of an S. S. guard (Kirsch) stationed at Dachau, who was arrested when the camp was liberated by American forces on April 29, 1945. [Photograph #49666]

Jubilant Belgians sit on top of a tank and celebrate the liberation of Brussels. [Photograph #65982]

Survivors take down the Nazi eagle that hangs above the entrance to the SS compound in Mauthausen on the day of liberation. The white car belongs to the Red Cross. [Photograph #07765]

Albanians view two cannons being towed by trucks during a military parade marking the liberation of Tirana. [Photograph #24736]

Pile of deceased prisoners in the Dachau concentration camp, found near the crematorium. Original caption reads: "Dachau Atrocity Camp: Stacked like cordwood, naked bodies of inmates of the infamous Dachau concentration camp were awaiting cremation when the 7th U." [Photograph #49660]

Liberated prisoners greet American soldiers at Allach, a sub-camp of Dachau. Original caption reads: "In prison stockade at Dachau, prisoners cheer the liberating Americans, who freed them from the inhuman treatment of the SS. [Photograph #49653]

Newly liberated prisoners stand around a mass grave at Dachau concentration camp. Original caption reads: "The prisoners show where they buried some of the comrades everyday, the ones who could not withstand the cruel treatment and starvation diet handed out by their German keepers." [Photograph #49663]

Remains of deceased prisoners found in the barracks of the Dachau concentration camp after liberation. Original caption reads: "The dead of the Dachau concentration camp lie in the back of the prison barracks." [Photograph #49661]

Emaciated body of a prisoner at Landsberg, found by the liberating American 7th Army. Original caption reads: "The Landsberg Atrocity: The emaciated bodies of Jewish prisoners bear evidence of the slow death by starvation they were undergoing before having been locked in their wooden huts by retreating Nazi prison guards, who set the huts afire and left." [Photograph #49655]

View of the still smoldering barracks at the Landsberg (Kaufering Lager I) sub-camp of Dachau concentration camp. Original caption reads: "Landsberg Atrocity: The emaciated bodies of victims of German cruelty at Landsberg prison." [Photograph #49657]

The bodies of burned prisoners lie in the rubble of the barracks at Landsberg. Original caption reads: "Pile of bodies which will be carried by German civilians from the town of Landsberg, Germany, and buried in graves also dug by German civilians in Stalag #4 Concentration Camp at Landsberg." [Photograph #49656]

An American soldier follows others into the still smoldering ruins of the Landsberg (Kaufering Lager I) concentration camp, sub-camp of Dachau. Original caption reads: "Landsberg atrocity: 7th U." [Photograph #49654]

Supreme Allied Expeditionary Force Commander, General Dwight D. Eisenhower, poses beneath the Arc de Triomphe with ranking French, British and American officers during a ceremony celebrating the liberation of Paris. [Photograph #37473]

Inmates waving a home-made American flag greet U. S. Seventh Army troops upon their arrival at the Allach concentration camp. Three survivors pictured in the photo are: Martin Kaufman (b. [Photograph #74599]

Mug shot of Hans Kurt Eisle, a physician stationed at Dachau, who was arrested when the camp was liberated by American forces on April 29, 1945. [Photograph #49680]

Mug shot of an S. S. guard (Witterler) stationed at Dachau, who was arrested when the camp was liberated by American forces on April 29, 1945. [Photograph #49667]

General Henning Linden, assistant commanding general, 42nd Rainbow Infantry Division, confers with various officials during the liberation and surrender of the Dachau concentration camp. [Photograph #08916]

Standing on a chair in the middle of Hagen Street in Eibergen, a local resident delivers a speech at a public celebration of the liberation of eastern Holland. [Photograph #37342]

Survivors celebrate their liberation from Amersfoort concentration camp. [Photograph #44959]

Dutch and Jewish children who had been in hiding pose together on liberation day. Rachel Kats is in the center. [Photograph #27259]

Mug shot of an S. S. guard (Becher) stationed at Dachau, who was arrested when the camp was liberated by American forces on April 29, 1945. [Photograph #49683]

Mug shot of an S. S. guard (Eichberger) stationed at Dachau, who was arrested when the camp was liberated by American forces on April 29, 1945. [Photograph #49675]

Mug shot of an S. S. guard (Tempel) stationed at Dachau, who was arrested when the camp was liberated by American forces on April 29, 1945. [Photograph #49669]

Mauthausen survivors cheer the soldiers of the Eleventh Armored Division of the U. S. Third Army one day after their actual liberation. The banner reads: "The Spanish Anti-Fascists Salute the Liberating Forces." [Photograph #68210]

Mug shot of an S. S. guard (Puhr) stationed at Dachau, who was arrested when the camp was liberated by American forces on April 29, 1945. [Photograph #49676]

Portrait of Marcel Tragholz (donor) and one of the American troops who liberated him in Belgium. [Photograph #29518]

Pile of prisoners clothing found near the crematorium in the Dachau concentration camp. Original caption reads: "Dachau Atrocity Camp: Tattered clothes from prisoners who were forced to strip before they were killed, lay in huge piles in the infamous Dachau concentration camp which was liberated by the 7th U." [Photograph #49659]

Document decorated with different shields and flags commemorates the liberation of Enschede by British and Canadian forces on April 1, 1945. [Photograph #43148]

Female survivors gather outside a barracks in the newly liberated Lenzing concentration camp. [Photograph #62767]

Portrait of two female survivors at the newly liberated Lenzing concentration camp. Pictured are Cesie Birnbaum (born 1922) from Poland and Milanie Herz (born 1920) in Slovakia. [Photograph #62765]

Female survivors gather outside a barracks in the newly liberated Lenzing concentration camp. [Photograph #62766]

A group of female survivors stands outside a barracks in the newly liberated Lenzing concentration camp. [Photograph #62764]

The French liaison arrives at the podium erected for a memorial funeral in the Buchenwald concentration camp after liberation. Orignial caption reads: "The arrival of an officer of the French liaison." [Photograph #23840]

Survivors waving flags of different nationalities flock to an outdoor Jewish memorial service in the liberated Dachau concentration camp. [Photograph #71078]

View of a monument/tombstone placed in Bergen-Belsen after the liberation on April 15, 1945 in memory of Jewish victims. The original caption states, "A monument erected in the camp in memory of the Jews who died there." [Photograph #44593]

Survivors gather in Buchenwald's main courtyard for the first burial procession at the camp. Orignial caption reads: "The first burial procession held at Buchenwald's main courtyard." [Photograph #23841]

American chaplain Rabbi Hershel Schaecter conducts Second Passover services for Buchenwald survivors shortly after liberation. Pictured in the first row wearing shorts is Robert Buechler, while the youth sitting in front of the lecturn, looking back at the camera, is Stefan Jakubowicz. [Photograph #26278]

Funeral procession in the Bindermichl displaced persons camp. [Photograph #41322]

Exterior view of a barrack in Ebelsberg DP camp. The camp was formerly used for American military personnel. [Photograph #04423]

View of one of the Salzburg displaced persons camps. [Photograph #82974]

Portrait of three young people in the Bindermichl displaced persons' camp in Linz, Austria. [Photograph #23654]

Group portrait of survivors in an unidentified camp (possibly Ebensee) soon after liberation. [Photograph #42512]

Jewish DPs protest against British immigration policy in Palestine at the Bad Gastein displaced persons camp. [Photograph #38243]

Group portrait of Jewish DPs at the New Palestine displaced persons camp. [Photograph #08716]

A crowd of people surrounded by police gathers in the Bindermichl displaced persons' camp in Linz, Austria. [Photograph #23655]

Survivors showing their tattoos after the liberation of Buchenwald. The lender's handwritten caption reads, "Two men showing numbers branded on arms. All clothing was also stamped where it was readily seen." [Photograph #78562A]

Two men pose next to a sign outside the Bindermichl displaced persons' camp in Linz, Austria. [Photograph #23653]

A group of Jewish displaced persons stands next to a sign outside the Bindermichl camp in Linz, Austria. [Photograph #23652]

Robert Fitterman is the author of over 12 books of poetry, including his long poem *Metropolis*, which has been published in 4 volumes: *Metropolis 1-15* (Sun & Moon Press, 2000), *Metropolis 16-29* (Coach House Books, 2002), *Metropolis XXX: The Decline and Fall of the Roman Empire* (Edge Books, 2004) and *Sprawl: Metropolis 30A* (Make Now Books, 2009). Fitterman's other titles include: *No Wait. Yep. Definitely Still Hate Myself* (Ugly Duckling Press, forthcoming 2014), *Rob's Word Shop* (Ugly Duckling Press, forthcoming 2014), *now we are friends* (Truck Books, 2010), *Rob the Plagiarist* (Roof Books, 2009), *war, the musical* (Subpress, 2006), and *Notes On Conceptualisms*, co-authored with Vanessa Place (Ugly Duckling Presse, 2009). His writing has been described as: *radical appropriation that aims to critique institutions by repurposing the languages of those institutions (e.g. corporate, network, consumerist)*. He is also the founder of Collective Task—a collective of over 30 international artists and writers who complete monthly "tasks" assigned by its members. He teaches writing and poetry at New York University and at the Bard College, Milton Avery School of Graduate Studies.